How to Counsel from Scripture

How to Counsel from Scripture

by
Martin and Deidre Bobgan

May the Lord encourage each person who reads this book,

Martin and Deidre Bobgan

MOODY PRESS
CHICAGO

Library of Congress Cataloging-in-Publication Data

Bobgan, Martin, 1930-
    How to counsel from Scripture.

    Bibliography: p.
    1. Peer counseling in the church.   2. Bible—
Psychology.   I. Bobgan, Deidre, 1935-   .   II. Title.
BV4409. B63   1985   235.5   85-18926
ISBN 0-8024-0373-5 (pbk.)

Printed in the United States of America

About this book . . .

The Bobgans have done it again! In readable form and with cogent arguments they have shown that to be Christian counseling must be scriptural. You will be both encouraged and instructed in reading this volume. Thank God for laymen like them.

JAY E. ADAMS
Dean of the Institute of Pastoral Studies
Christian Counseling and Educational Foundation
Professor of Practical Theology
Westminster Theological Seminary

The Bobgans have written a most challenging book, especially for those who are Christian psychologists. The authors propose a non-fee charging and pure Scripture-based model of counseling. They directly challenge the typical Christian psychologist whose practice is modeled largely on the concepts and procedures of secular psychotherapy. Their position is radical and I don't agree with all their views, but there is a great deal of uncomfortable truth in what they are saying—truth that many in the field of Christian psychology need to confront honestly.

PAUL C. VITZ
Professor of Psychology
New York University

Psychological counseling is one of the greatest seductions in Christianity today. The Bobgans have not only exposed this deception but have called the church back to its biblical responsibility to "bear one another's burdens and so fulfill the law of Christ." I strongly recommend this book to every Christian pastor and enthusiastically encourage every Christian lay person to read it and to follow its message.

DAVE HUNT
Author and Cult Researcher

To W. Phillip Keller, who has
consistently elevated the Lord and His
Word and inspired many to love and
obey God

Contents

Foreword

The Christian church of the late twentieth century stands in peril from the impact of psychotherapy. This pseudoscience devised by the non-Christian minds of men like Freud has deceived not only the worldly society of our times, but also many within the community of Christ.

More and more there has arisen an enormous need for enlightened Christian leaders to alert their fellows to this danger. No longer can the church remain silent when its leaders, instead of bringing men and women to Christ for healing, refer them to those using psychotherapy or psychological techniques for cure.

This book, like its predecessor *The Psychological Way/ The Spiritual Way*, is a clarion call to God's people to turn from humanistic methods of curing men's souls back to the Great Physician Himself. It is a ringing cry of warning that our hope lies not in man's ways, but in the magnificent life and love of God Himself.

It is of more than passing significance that this word of warning should come from concerned lay people. It comes at a crucial point in the history of the church when more and more its pulpits are being occupied by predators—wolves in sheep's wool—pretending to speak for God while in reality advocating the world's ways.

Its message will not be popular—the prophets who speak the truth of God's revelation never are. But it can be potent for those who heed it. Its counsel and direction are clear, sound, and wise with the insights of God's own gracious Spirit.

This volume should be required reading for pastors, teachers, and lay leaders entrusted with the care of men's souls.

W. PHILLIP KELLER

Acknowledgments

We are grateful to the pastors and lay people who have worked with us in the ministry of biblical counseling. We particularly mention Jim Harmon, Teele Manning, Florie Matthews, and Gene Whitlach, the lay counselors who reviewed the manuscript and confirmed again the efficacy of biblical counseling. Also, we greatly thank Jay Adams for his thorough reading, important suggestions, and sound advice. In addition we thank Tom McMahon who has prodded us along and made a number of suggestions. Finally, we are indebted to W. Phillip Keller for sharing his wisdom, specific suggestions, and great encouragement.

Introduction

In our book *The Psychological Way/The Spiritual Way* we questioned the use of psychological counseling (psychotherapy) and encouraged a return to biblical counseling. We gave authoritative evidence that psychotherapy is questionable at best, detrimental at worst, and a spiritual counterfeit at least. In view of the research, which has not demonstrated the superiority of psychological counseling, our greatest concern is that the cure of minds (the psychological way) has displaced the cure of souls (the spiritual way) until the latter is almost absent from the church.

Today the greatest single obstacle to biblical counseling is psychological counseling and all it pretends to be. The primary reason churches do not minister to mental-emotional-behavioral problems is because of fear—fear that individuals who are not formally trained cannot handle such problems and fear that criticism might be directed at the church for even trying. Since that fear seems to be so universal, we are compelled to deal with the psychological way of counseling as we present the spiritual way. Our criticism is not an attack on all of psychology. We criticize only that portion of psychology that claims to help individuals with their mental-emotional-behavioral problems.

Just as Jeremiah lamented over Israel's looking to other gods to alleviate its problems, we are concerned that God's people are looking to an empty, man-made conglomeration of psychological systems of counseling.

> For my people have committed two evils:
> They have forsaken Me,
> The fountain of living waters,
> To hew for themselves cisterns,
> Broken cisterns,
> That can hold no water.
>   (Jeremiah 2:13)

This book is for the Christian who wants to know more about counseling the spiritual way. Biblical counseling involves change, choice, and love. God desires to transform us into the image of Christ. Lack of change is an indication of spiritual stagnation, and being transformed into the image of Christ is a sign of spiritual vitality.

Life's experiences can motivate people to change in different directions. But the change that comes out of the conversation called counseling must be a biblically oriented change, which involves the work of God and the response of the individual. For change to occur, there must be a choice. God created each person with responsibility for choices. And a biblical choice is necessary for change in the proper direction. In this book we give an overview of the human condition out of which choice occurs and present some ways in which choice can be encouraged.

As we discuss the biblical model of man and methodology of change, the one force of Scripture on which we focus is the love of God. God's love enables one to overcome sin and its consequences, to live in relationship to Him, and to be transformed into the image of Christ. His love engenders trust, which leads to obedience to His Word. God's love includes both His mercy and truth, both His grace and justice. In biblical counseling the love of God is ministered in a balance of mercy and truth to provide both a supportive environment and direction for change. For counseling to be truly biblical, love must be its hallmark, its means, and its direction because "God is love." Since love is such a predominant factor in change, we show several facets of it as a basis for counseling.

As we discuss the framework for a biblical counseling ministry, present a biblical model of man and methodology of change, and elaborate on counseling principles found throughout Scripture, you may discover that you already have a counseling ministry in your church. But unless we seek in counseling a spiritual understanding (biblical model of man) and spiritual solutions (biblical methodology), we are doing a great injustice to the counselee at least and a great damage at worst. Problems of living must be dealt with as spiritual problems with spiritual solutions.

At no time do we wish to give the impression that biblical counseling can be reduced to formulas. Those who counsel by formulas will fail, or they will succeed for reasons other than the formulas used. Any formulized biblical counseling will fall short of what true biblical counseling is—a creative, spiritual process involving a person who needs help and another person who will come alongside as God's channel of mercy and truth.

The framework we offer is just one small glimpse of what is totally available in Scripture; it is not complete, nor can it be. Each person who comes to counseling is unique, and God will minister in a unique way to that individual. The Scriptures and the Holy Spirit provide an infinite number of possible applications of truth to be ministered in love to each person in each situation. The biblical counselor attempts to be sensitive to the individual and to the Holy Spirit as he discusses or demonstrates biblical principles. If one were to take a biblical principle and apply it without regard for the counselee's readiness to receive or without being in harmony with God's work in a person's life, then even biblical principles may lead to disaster. It is possible to use the Bible and be wrong, and it is possible to quote the Bible and interfere with the work of God. Therefore, biblical counseling is a spiritual activity that combines the Word of God and the work of the Holy Spirit through one who is called to counsel and to one who will receive it.

Some persons who come in for counseling are experiencing more than merely the ordinary problems of living and need medical help beyond what the counselor can give. Furthermore, research indicates that certain types of severe cases are biological disorders which require medical help. (See chapter 16 on "Warnings.") Yet though we urge that the counselor refer patients with biological disorders to medical doctors, we claim as well that for those persons in mental distress who do not suffer from organic brain disorder or serious chemical imbalance, the type of counseling we propose is of far greater benefit than any other we know of.

Recently a woman described to us what had happened when she and her husband had decided against biblical counseling. After a year and a half of psychological counseling, their marriage ended in divorce. But then they both turned back to the Lord for direction and help. As they sought His will in their lives and moved in the direction of relationship with Him, they began reestablishing their relationship with each other. She concluded by saying, "You know, Jesus Christ really is the answer to life's problems!" Her words and all that they imply are the premise upon which this book and our counseling ministry rest.

We pray that as you read this book, you will find encouragement to seek the springs of living water for yourself and for others. The Word of God and the work of the Holy Spirit provide power for overcoming the problems of living. Biblical counseling needs to be restored in churches immediately before more Christians are sent to an alien world for help. Pastors and lay people who have this call of God on their hearts *can* begin a counseling ministry—not next month or next year, but now. The gift of counseling has been given to edify the church and to glorify God.

> As each one has received a special gift, employ it in serving one another, as good stewards of the manifold grace of God. Whoever speaks, let him speak, as it were, the utterances of God; whoever serves, let him do so as by the strength which God supplies; so that in all things God may be glorified through Jesus Christ, to whom belongs the glory and dominion forever and ever. Amen. (1 Peter 4:10–11)

PART 1

Model and Methodology for Change

1

The Cure of Souls

From its very beginning the Christian church had a method and ministry for dealing with mental-emotional-behavioral problems. Through what was known as the "cure of souls," counsel was given to minister in the areas of emotions, thoughts, values, attitudes, relationships, and behavior. John T. McNeill, in his book *A History of the Cure of Souls*, describes this ministry as "the sustaining and curative treatment of persons in those matters that reach beyond the requirements of the animal life."[1] Until the twentieth century both the Roman Catholic and Protestant churches provided personal ministry to those in need. Therefore, spiritual, biblical counseling is not a new idea. We are merely promoting a restoration of one of the oldest ministries, which is a ministry of love.

God heals people who have been hurt and forgives those who have sinned and repented. The cure-of-souls ministry emphasized the person's relationship with God from which comes renewal and change in the mental-emotional-behavioral areas of life.

God has instructed and prepared Christians to care for each other and to encourage growth. But the world systems have undermined the cure-of-souls ministry and intimidated Christians in such a way that they feel unable to help. Even pastors have felt unquali-

1. John T. McNeill, *A History of the Cure of Souls* (New York: Harper & Row, 1951), p. vii.

fied because the world has set up systems, requirements, degrees, and licenses which say who is qualified to counsel, even though such ministry in the church is a calling of God and a gift of grace.

The flow of personal care and counsel has been blocked by outside systems that have yet to prove themselves as scientific or more effective than the cure-of-souls ministry. Thus many Christians believe that only superficial problems can be handled by the church and that more complex problems are beyond its grasp. When the problems go beyond the ordinary, when persons are really experiencing pain and misery, when they reach the level at which a simple answer does not suffice, the church fears to become involved. Pastors have felt inadequate and too overwhelmed with other responsibilities to help in difficult situations. As a result, Christians have been sent elsewhere.

Many Christians seek help from their pastors before looking elsewhere. In fact the Joint Commission on Mental Illness and Health, through a national survey, found that nearly half of all individuals needing counseling went to a clergyman first.[2] But rather than receiving help within the church, such individuals are generally referred to the psychological counselor's office or else ignored. Without the use of research and through the myth and mystique of professional counseling, the church has been deceived into abandoning its call to guide and help Christians who most desperately need counsel and transformation.

TO WHOM CAN THE CHURCH MINISTER?

Who can benefit from biblical counseling within the church? Research psychiatrist E. Fuller Torrey says that about 5 percent of those who come to a psychiatrist are people with organic brain disease, about 75 percent are people with problems of living, and the other 20 percent "will require closer examination to make a final judgment."[3] Torrey suggests that the majority (at least 75 percent) of those who come to a psychiatrist actually need to be educated in how to live. They do not need to receive treatment.[4]

George Albee, past president of the American Psychological Association, says: "The unvarnished fact is that most of the emo-

---

2. Joint Commission on Mental Illness and Health, *Action for Mental Health* (New York: Science Editions, 1961), p. 103.
3. E. Fuller Torrey, *The Death of Psychiatry* (Radnor, Pa.: Chilton, 1974), p. 195.
4. Ibid., part 2.

tional problems of living do not belong in the category of disease."[5]
Authors of *The Madness Establishment* state:

> It is clear that out of the tens of millions of individuals whom NIMH
> [National Institute of Mental Health] officials and others estimate need
> psychiatric care, only a tiny minority suffer from problems that most
> authorities would agree constitute "mental diseases."[6]

Therefore, most people seeking help need the kind of counsel in
which the Bible excels: how to live, how to relate to others, how to
find meaning in life, how to know God, and how to become the kind
of person God wants.

WHO CAN BEST MINISTER?

If most psychiatric clients actually need to be taught how to live,
who is better equipped to guide and teach than the man or woman of
God? (Furthermore, how can an individual separated from the Body
of Christ be equipped to teach a Christian how to live?) Nevertheless,
most psychiatrists and other psychotherapists would not want to lose
such clients, since they actually prefer working with those who
would most likely benefit from biblical counseling. Torrey reports:

> Another peculiarity of psychiatrists as "doctors" is that they avoid the
> really "sick patients." Instead, they spend the vast majority of their
> time with those "patients" who are least "sick." This is certainly a
> curious way to practice medicine.[7]

In fact, many psychotherapists rarely even see patients outside of
those who are experiencing problems of living.[8] Psychiatrist Jerome
Frank confesses that "if troubled people were to be excluded from
our offices, there would be very little left of our practices."[9]
    The psychotherapist often gives commonsense advice that is
sanctified by his title and his secular training. For example, in

5. George Albee, letter to editor, *APA Monitor* 8, no. 2 (February 1977): 2.
6. Franklin Chu and Sharland Trotter, *The Madness Establishment* (New York:
   Grossman, 1974), p. 206.
7. Torrey, p. 58.
8. Ibid., chap. 10.
9. Jerome Frank, "Mental Health in a Fragmented Society: The Shattered Crystal
   Ball," *American Journal of Orthopsychiatry* 49, no. 3 (July 1979): 406.

counseling about bringing a friend to one's parents' house, a Del Mar, California psychiatrist advised: "And don't set up a situation you know ahead of time is not going to work. If you're bringing home a 6-foot-8 black basketball player and your parents are racist, you know that's not going to work."[10] Perhaps a few people would not have enough sense to know that, but why send a person to school for five to ten years just to charge money for dispensing such advice?

Psychiatrist Thomas Szasz refers to the "transformation of the ordinary behaviors of ordinary people into extraordinary and awe-inspiring symptoms of mental diseases."[11] And William Kilpatrick, in his book *Psychological Seduction*, tells us the results: "Real human problems are trivialized by reducing them to pathologies, thus robbing our everyday struggles of any dignity or meaning."[12]

Paul Vitz says:

> What does one say to the older worker who has lost his job, whose skills are not wanted? What does one tell the woman who is desperately alone inside an aging body and with a history of failed relationships? Does one advise such people to become more autonomous and independent? Does one say "go actualize yourself in creative activity"? For people in those circumstances such advice is not just irrelevant, it is an insult.[13]

Kilpatrick aptly describes modern psychological help:

> If you are looking for new worlds to explore, you had best look beyond psychology. It has the illusion of depth, but then so do facing mirrors, and I am afraid psychology is very much like one of those hall of mirrors you find in an amusement park. You get to see different facets and reflections of yourself, but that is all you see. A hall of mirrors is in reality only a room, and sooner or later you will want to find your way out. You will want to find a door.[14]

---

10. Harold Bloomfield, in "Psychiatrist Says Holiday with Family Needn't Be Turkey," *Santa Barbara News Press*, 23 November 1983, p. A-3.
11. Thomas Szasz, *The Myth of Psychotherapy* (Garden City, N.Y.: Doubleday, Anchor, 1978), p. 194.
12. William Kirk Kilpatrick, *Psychological Seduction* (Nashville: Thomas Nelson, 1983), p. 190.
13. Paul C. Vitz, *Psychology as Religion: The Cult of Self-Worship* (Grand Rapids: Eerdmans, 1977), p. 104.
14. Kilpatrick, p. 227.

He also says, "The trouble with psychology is not that it incites our imagination and passions but that it finally deadens them."[15]

How strange that psychotherapists have been elevated to the position of expertise in matters of living. The high divorce, suicide, and burn-out rates among psychotherapists indicate the fragmentation that underlies many of their personal lives and professional practices, and yet people look to them for wisdom in how to live happily and successfully.[16]

The church can certainly better assume the responsibility of teaching individuals how to live. "Seeing that His divine power has granted to us everything pertaining to life and godliness, through the true knowledge of Him who called us by His own glory and excellence" (2 Peter 1:3). The church has the Scriptures and believers who can minister love in mercy and truth to those facing problems of living.

Ministers should not send members of their flock elsewhere for counsel, nor should they try to emulate psychological counselors. Paul did not choose to follow the ways of men when he said that he preached "not with enticing words of man's wisdom, but in demonstration of the Spirit and of power; that your faith should not stand in the wisdom of men, but in the power of God" (1 Corinthians 2:4-5, KJV*). Pastors cannot expect to carry the full burden of personal counsel. Rather, they need to instruct members of the local church how to help one another, how to bear one another's burdens, and how to counsel in mercy and truth.

The research presented in *The Psychological Way/The Spiritual Way*, along with the experience we have had in developing and directing a counseling ministry in our church, has led us to the following conclusion: *For Christians, problems that can be treated by psychological counseling can be better ministered to by biblical counsel within the Body of Christ.* Research psychiatrist Torrey says,

> Spiritual counseling is as valid and effective a way to assist people who have problems of living, and is in fact more honest . . . than most. For

---

* King James Version.
15. Ibid., p. 229.
16. E. Fuller Torrey, "Hollywood's Pique at Psychiatry," *Psychology Today*, July 1981, p. 79.

people with problems of living who share the Bobgans' spiritual world view, their approach would be the most effective.[17]

But instead of providing biblical ministry and counsel, the church has promoted psychological counseling, perhaps without being aware of the grave differences between the two.

WHY BIBLICAL COUNSELING RATHER THAN PSYCHOLOGICAL COUNSELING?

We firmly believe that even in cases of bio-chemical illness where a medical doctor has been called in to assist in treatment there is no reason to turn to psychological counseling or to an amalgamation of biblical and psychological counseling. The Word of God and the work of the Holy Spirit are sufficient to transform the problems of living and can do so with no help from psychological theories or techniques. After thoroughly researching the usefulness of the cure of minds (psychotherapy), we state without hesitation that the church should altogether avoid any alliance with it. For almost two-thousand years the church did without the pseudoscience of psychotherapy and still was able to minister successfully to those burdened by the problems of living.

When the Word of God, ministered through the Holy Spirit, touches a person's spirit, his thinking, feeling, and acting are affected. To change thought, emotion, and behavior in the absence of the Word of God and the work of the Holy Spirit will ultimately exalt the wisdom of man rather than the truth and Spirit of God.

There are four major reasons we do not recommend psychological counseling or a combination of psychological and biblical counseling: First, because of the Bible itself and the tradition of the church; second, because of the experiences of those who use only a biblical approach; third, because of psychological research; and fourth, because of the psychological way's inherent interference with the biblical way.

THE BIBLE AND TRADITION

The Bible exhorts us to "bear one another's burdens, and thus fulfill the law of Christ" (Galatians 6:2). Many other verses encour-

17. E. Fuller Torrey, endorsement of Martin Bobgan and Deidre Bobgan, *The Psychological Way/The Spiritual Way* (Minneapolis: Bethany Fellowship, 1979), cover.

age Christians to exhort one another and to help one another with difficulties. The Bible also teaches about right thinking and acting and about human emotions and volition. As a result of such teachings, the cure-of-souls ministry was established early in the church and existed right up to the twentieth century. But now psychological counseling has become dominant.

Szasz points out that with "the decline of religion and the growth of science . . . the cure of (sinful) souls, which had been an integral part of the Christian religions, was recast as the cure of (sick) minds."[18] The words *sinful* and *sick* in parentheses are his. These two words mark the dramatic shift from the cure of souls to the cure of minds (psychotherapy). Once we make sin a sickness, we transform a biblical problem into a psychological problem. The resulting consequence is to move problems of living from the loving hands of the pastor to the office of the professional practitioner. Elsewhere Szasz points out that "the human relations we now call 'psychotherapy' are matters of religion—and that we mislabel them as 'therapeutic' at great risk to our spiritual well-being."[19] He further says, "Psychotherapy is a modern scientific-sounding name for what used to be called the 'cure of souls.'"[20] But psychotherapy's "cure of souls" is anything but biblical.

Although the church has nearly abandoned biblical counseling because of the so-called scientific nature of psychological counseling, psychological counseling is not any more scientific than biblical counseling. Karl Popper, who is one of the most influential thinkers of our day and one of the greatest philosophers of science, believes that psychological theories such as those formulated by Sigmund Freud and others "though posing as sciences, had in fact more in common with primitive myths than with science; that they resembled astrology rather than astronomy."[21] Thus, the takeover of spiritual counseling by psychological counseling cannot be justified on the grounds of science.

BIBLICAL COUNSELING

Although psychological counseling is the predominant method used in and out of the church today for problems of living, biblical

18. Szasz, p. xxiv.
19. Thomas Szasz, endorsement of Bobgan and Bobgan, *The Psychological Way/The Spiritual Way*, cover.
20. Szasz, *The Myth of Psychotherapy*, p. 26.
21. Karl Popper, "Scientific Theory and Falsifiability," in *Perspectives in Philosophy*, ed. Robert N. Beck (New York: Holt, Rinehart, and Winston, 1975), p. 343.

counseling ministries do exist across America. One outstanding example is the Christian Counseling and Educational Foundation, which was founded by Jay Adams. These ministries successfully deal with the same problems of living as are handled with psychological counseling. The existence of such ministries does not answer the question of which method is more effective, but it does demonstrate that some ministers and counselors successfully use the Bible rather than a system of psychotherapy.

RESEARCH OF PSYCHOLOGICAL COUNSELING

The third case against psychological counseling is found in research literature. Morris Parloff, chief of the Psychosocial Treatment Research Branch of the National Institute of Mental Health, after evaluating a vast amount of research, refers to the "disconcerting finding that all forms of psychotherapy appear to be equally effective."[22] Researchers from Wesleyan University came to an even more startling conclusion: that there is no evidence that the benefits of psychotherapy are greater than "even the most seemingly innocuous nonpsychotherapeutic treatments."[23] Logic would lead us to conclude that since biblical counseling involves all the essential kinds of ingredients of psychotherapy (such as a model of man and methodology of change), it would do at least as well as the more than 250 methods of psychological treatment.

Even before the rise of psychological treatment, there was a method of cure referred to in the literature as "moral treatment."[24] The moral treatment, which was used in institutions for persons suffering from mental-emotional problems, yielded similar cure rates to what present-day psychotherapy claims. Hans Eysenck reports that, when he investigated the records of the hospital in England where he works, even the seventeenth-century cure rates were equivalent to present claims for professional treatment.[25] If moral treatment of the past did as well as present psychological treatment,

22. Morris Parloff, "Psychotherapy and Research: An Anaclitic Depression," *Psychiatry* 43 (November 1980): 287.
23. Leslie Prioleau, Martha Murdock, and Nathan Brody, "An Analysis of Psychotherapy Versus Placebo Studies," *The Behavioral and Brain Sciences* 6 (June 1983): 275.
24. Ronald L. Koteskey, "Abandoning the Psyche to Secular Treatment," *Christianity Today*, 29 June 1979, p. 20.
25. Hans Eysenck, "Psychotherapy, Behavior Therapy and the Outcome Problem." BMA Audio Cassette (New York: Guilford, n.d.).

then why wouldn't biblical counseling do as well? The startling fact is that no one has ever compared biblical and psychological counseling, and thus no one really knows whether psychological counseling is any better than biblical counseling. To put it more succinctly, no one at any time has ever shown that psychological counseling is one whit better than biblical counseling. Nevertheless, many in the church have been deluded into thinking that it is.

INTERFERENCE OF THE PSYCHOLOGICAL WAY

Christianity is easily neutralized by substituting the Word of God with psychotherapeutic theories and teachings. Rather than building Christian character and conscience, psychotherapy builds any number of substitutes, from humanistic benevolence to self-centeredness. To send people out of the church for psychological counseling is to risk referring them to another philosophy, another moral system.

If people solve their problems of living with the wisdom of men, they will tend to draw closer to self rather than closer to God. Faith in the psychological way leads to the worship of man rather than God. One psychotherapist confesses:

> Psychology has become something of a substitute for old belief systems. Different schools of therapy offer visions of the good life and how to live it, and those whose ancestors took comfort from the words of God and worshipped at the altars of Christ and Yahweh now take solace from and worship at the altars of Freud, Jung, Carl Rogers, Albert Ellis, Werner Erhard, and a host of similar authorities.[26]

To combine biblical counseling with forms of counseling which have been offered as a substitute salvation seems quite contradictory.

Both the psychological way and the spiritual way of counseling deal with thought and behavior. Nevertheless, the psychological way neatly reduces Christianity to a religious realm that has nothing to do with really helping people change thought and behavior. Psychotherapists claim to have the expertise and training to help individuals solve problems of thinking and behaving and confine religion to the realm of the spirit—"somewhere beyond the realities of everyday

26. Bernie Zilbergeld, *The Shrinking of America: Myths of Psychological Change* (Boston: Little, Brown, 1983), p. 5.

life." Jacob Needleman notes this shift from the cure-of-souls ministry to the psychotherapist's domain:

> Modern psychiatry arose out of the vision that man must change himself and not depend for help upon an imaginary God. Over half a century ago, mainly through the insights of Freud and through the energies of those he influenced, the human psyche was wrested from the faltering hands of organized religion and was situated in the world of nature as a subject for scientific study.[27]

Martin Gross, in his book *The Psychological Society,* says:

> When educated man lost faith in formal religion, he required a substitute belief that would be as reputable in the last half of the twentieth century as Christianity was in the first. Psychology and psychiatry have now assumed that special role.[28]

In his book *Psychological Seduction,* Kilpatrick warns:

> True Christianity does not mix well with psychology. When you try to mix them, you often end up with a watered-down Christianity instead of a Christianized psychology. But the process is subtle and is rarely noticed. I wasn't aware that I was confusing two different things. And others in the church who might have been expected to put me right were under the same enchantment as I. It was not a frontal attack on Christianity—I'm sure I would have resisted that. It was not a case of a wolf at the door: the wolf was already in the fold, dressed in sheep's clothing. And from the way it was petted and fed by some of the shepherds, one would think it was the prize sheep.[29]

During this century the soul has been reduced to mind, the mind has been confused with the brain, and the church has relegated mental-emotional distress and problems of living to professional practitioners who specialize in the mind "sciences." Separating the mind from the spirit leads to the erroneous conclusion that the Bible is incapable of dealing with problems of thinking and behaving.

27. Jacob Needleman, "Psychiatry and the Sacred," in *Consciousness: Brain, States of Awareness, and Mysticism,* ed. Daniel Goleman and Richard J. Davidson (New York: Harper & Row, 1979), p. 209.
28. Martin L. Gross, *The Psychological Society* (New York: Random House, 1978), p. 9.
29. Kilpatrick, p. 23.

Both the psychological way and the spiritual way provide nonscientific solutions to mental-emotional-behavioral problems. The spiritual way provides biblical solutions; the psychological way provides man-made solutions.

The psychological way, claiming to be scientific, is practiced as a profession. The spiritual way is a natural outflow of Christian love practiced in the Body of Christ. The psychological way requires training in the theories and techniques devised by men. Only designated, trained individuals may offer professional psychological help. The spiritual way, on the other hand, may be practiced by members of the Body of Christ. Biblical counseling is not based on the theories or techniques of men, but rather is practiced by those who know the Bible, have applied God's Word in their own lives by the enabling of the Holy Spirit, and love others in such a way as to minister healing and life.

The Bible is filled with information about the condition of humanity and with teachings that lead to emotional stability and power for living. The information presented in this book only begins to tap the treasure of the inexhaustible riches in the Word of God. As one continues to study Scripture as a text for counseling and seeks particular guidance from the Holy Spirit, he will find what he needs to lead people into the right kind of living. Christians have the whole counsel of God as they yield themselves to the Lord, as they read and obey the Word, and as they are indwelt and empowered by the Holy Spirit, who is the true Counselor.

God did not abandon mankind to the wiles of the devil and to a hostile world. He gave His only begotten Son, His written Word, His Holy Spirit, and fellow believers so that His children might know Him in such a way as to love Him, to trust Him, and to follow His design for living. Biblical counseling that follows the principles and patterns of Scripture, and particularly the highest commandments to love God and neighbor, is a more godly and consistent way to minister to Christians than are multitudes of psychotherapies. Not only may problems be solved, but an individual may draw closer to God, gain inner spiritual strength and stability, and become more and more like Jesus.

2

A Place for Change

Churches are made up of people in different places of growth and Christian experience. Although on the surface people may appear to be happy, some are suffering from difficult problems of living. Some are on the verge of divorce or are trying to recover from the devastation of fractured relationships and broken homes. Others have personal distresses such as anxiety, depression, fear, and anger.

The church has ministered to such problems since its inception. Jesus was the answer nearly two thousand years ago; He was the answer through the centuries; and He is the answer today for those who are suffering in their thoughts, emotions, and personal relationships. Jesus does have the answers, the solutions, and the power to reconstruct broken lives. He is still the One who fulfills the prophecy of Isaiah 61 by bringing good news to the afflicted, binding up the brokenhearted, and proclaiming liberty to the captives.

Jesus promised to be with His people in the midst of problems, to guide them through those hardships, and to strengthen and mold them as they endure the crucible of pain and distress. The Lord said in Isaiah 43:1b-3,

> Do not fear, for I have redeemed you;
> I have called you by name; you are Mine!
> When you pass through the waters, I will be with you;

When you walk through the fire, you will not be scorched,
Nor will the flame burn you.
For I am the Lord your God,
The Holy One of Israel, your Savior.

Jesus brings the healing of His nurturing and sustaining love. He is sensitive to people's needs and understands the problems of living. He yearns to minister His strength and love to each person, for He said,

> Come to Me, all who are weary and heavy-laden, and I will give you rest. Take My yoke upon you, and learn from Me, for I am gentle and humble in heart; and you shall find rest for your souls. For My yoke is easy, and My load is light. (Matthew 11:28-30)

Through mercy and truth Jesus teaches believers how to walk through life yoked with Him. They learn to live as Jesus lived, and they learn how to face and overcome the problems of living through His indwelling Spirit. Through a relationship of love, He enables them to live according to His life and His perfect will.

Just as Jesus loved His disciples and taught them how to live, He sent His Holy Spirit to continue His personal ministry in the life of each believer to accomplish spiritual growth and change. As a Christian encounters problems, Jesus is there by means of the Holy Spirit.

Furthermore, He has given His followers His written Word:

> All Scripture is inspired by God and profitable for teaching, for reproof, for correction, for training in righteousness; that the man of God may be adequate, equipped for every good work. (2 Timothy 3:16-17)

Jesus also provided a tangible, visible means by which to minister His healing and strengthening love to each person. He formed the church, which is His Body with eyes, ears, hands, and heart, to be filled by Him. He designed the church as a channel through which He could significantly touch the lives of those who are under the weight of heavy problems. He has called the body to assist people who are struggling with thoughts, emotions, and behavior that cause havoc in their lives.

Jesus created the church to minister His love. He called believers to love one another—and that means to care for each other, to bear one another's burdens, to build up one another in the faith. Jesus has gifted and called individuals in the body "for the equipping of the saints for the work of service, to the building up of the body of Christ" (Ephesians 4:12). When the church, the Body of Christ, is functioning correctly, truth will be ministered in such a way as to edify each believer.

> But speaking the truth in love, we are to grow up in all aspects into Him, who is the head, even Christ, from whom the whole body, being fitted and held together by that which every joint supplies, according to the proper working of each individual part, causes the growth of the body for the building up of itself in love. (Ephesians 4:15-16)

In the Body of Christ all are to minister and all are to receive ministry. Thus, one may at one time serve as a counselor, encourager, and helping friend, but at another time that same person may be on the receiving end. We are partners with the Lord through sharing the love of God.

The church is a fellowship of saints in the process of becoming like Jesus. Once a person is born of the Spirit through faith in Jesus, he begins a new life. Although the initial transformation takes place in a moment of time, the Christian continues to be changed as he yields his life to God. Jesus planned us to "attain to the unity of the faith, and of the knowledge of the Son of God, to a mature man, to the measure of the stature which belongs to the fulness of Christ" (Ephesians 4:13). The church, therefore, is meant to be a place' of change and growth by being a bodily expression of God's love.

The church provides opportunities for change through three basic levels of ministry: the large group, the small group, and person to person. The large-group ministry is mainly corporate worship with preaching and teaching of the Word for evangelism, instruction in how to live, and the edification of the entire body of believers. The small-group ministry is at a more personal level and serves to guide members in living and building one another in the faith. The person-to-person ministry includes any sharing and caring among members of the body and would include the ministry of spiritual counseling. These levels of ministry are not separate, but are intertwining, interdependent, and intersupportive. And biblical counseling is a part of all three ministries. A church that truly functions as the Body of Christ will include opportunities for growth at all three levels and will serve to deepen an individual's personal relationship with God.

LARGE-GROUP MINISTRY

The corporate worship and preaching of the Word are essential activities of a church. Through this broad ministry many lives are touched. If the teaching and preaching are biblically sound and communicated in love, and if the believers are responding, then many in the congregation will be growing spiritually and meeting life's problems in the context of God's love, which includes both His mercy and His truth.

Preaching and teaching provide opportunities for counsel from the Word. Every minister should be presenting valuable lessons from the Word that apply to daily living. So much of Scripture, properly taught, can have life-transforming effects. As a minister brings forth the love of God and applies His Word, lives will be changed.

SMALL-GROUP MINISTRY

Even in churches in which the Word is faithfully and accurately proclaimed and taught, there is a need for personal ministry within the church to communicate God's love and commitment to specific persons in their particular situations.

Much personal ministry may occur in small groups within the church. Such groups need to be centered on the love of God, on the teaching of the Word, on the fellowship of mutual care and concern, on being sensitive and responsive to each other as persons being formed by Christ, on bearing one another's burdens, and on prayer. When small groups meet in homes people get to know one another better and begin to share and worship together on a more intimate basis.

Larger churches especially find that small groups are essential for the expression of love in pertinent and practical ways. Love can be given in a general way in a large group setting. But when a member of the Body of Christ is really hurting, facing difficult trials and temptations, or working on important decisions, that person is better ministered to by the consistent, regular, through-the-week involvement a small group can provide.

As small groups follow the forms presented in Scripture rather than any adopted or adapted from humanistic systems, they can participate in Jesus' commandment to "love one another as I have loved you." A group leader would do well to search Scripture and seek the Lord in leading the group, rather than to learn techniques that might reduce the whole process to a sterile methodology. The small group should be the visible expression of the Body of Christ and therefore operate according to His character and Word. Praying for one another in the group leads to concern and help as members become sensitive to one another's needs. Believers begin loving each other, esteeming one another more than self, submitting to one another, encouraging each other, and rejoicing together as they come together for growth and change.

Because participation in the small group so enriches the large-group worship experience, every church should have this added ministry. Since every church needs a setting in which members can reach deeper levels of caring, we encourage pastors to make sure that they have a small-group ministry in their churches before even considering having a person-to-person counseling ministry. The best and most effective counseling one can give and receive can occur in Christ-centered small groups. It is our experience that 95 percent of the problems and potential problems of living faced by members of a church can be alleviated by the large and small-group ministries. A fellowship that loves God and neighbor as self will be the best antidote for trials, troubles, and tribulations.

Leonard Syme, a professor of epidemiology at the University of California at Berkeley, indicates the importance of social ties and social support systems in relationship to mortality and disease rates. He points to Japan as being number one in the world with respect to health and then discusses the close social, cultural, and traditional ties in that country as the reason. He believes that the more social ties, the better the health and the lower the death rate. Conversely, he indicates that the more isolated the person, the poorer the health and the higher the death rate.[1]

Social ties are good preventative medicine for physical problems and for mental-emotional-behavioral problems. In addition to being

---

1. Leonard Syme, "People Need People: Social Support and Health," *The Healing Brain* audio tape series, tape #12 (Los Altos, Calif.: Institute for the Study of Human Knowledge Book Service, 1981).

"an ounce of prevention," social ties can be "a pound of cure." Human love has always been a beneficial balm. But greater than this is the love of God expressed and received in a fellowship of believers.

PERSON-TO-PERSON MINISTRY

The person-to-person ministry of friendship and mutual concern exists in every church. These informal relationships provide opportunities to share God's love and to encourage one another through the trials of life. Though a church setting up a counseling program should provide some training, it is a fact that counseling occurs in all human relationships. We all counsel, and we all are counseled by others. Moreover, all believers are called to be channels of God's mercy and truth. One purpose of this book, therefore, is to encourage the continuation of these informal relationships and to show some effective principles for change.

The stronger and the greater the number and depth of person-to-person relationships, the less there is a need for a specific counseling ministry in a church. Therefore, a church should encourage to a maximum relationships that strengthen believers. Besides being in regular attendance in church services and being involved in a small group, individuals suffering through problems should be helped to find meaningful person-to-person relationships in the church so that support can be given.

Some members of the Body of Christ are not specifically involved with other believers or are not involved with at least one other person who can provide the care that is needed. These are the ones who need spiritual, biblical counseling that provides a helping relationship the person in need has not yet found. The care that is provided in such counseling involves the Word of God and the work of the Holy Spirit in the same way that occurs in biblical interpersonal relationships of all kinds.

One great error that has occurred in counseling in general is that people have made a mystique of the counseling relationship, when in truth it is just a formalized person-to-person relationship that happens because the person in need has no one in his own environment to turn to. Those who are effective in biblically helping others through informal relationships are usually effective in a specific person-to-person counseling ministry.

The principles mentioned in this book are effective in all biblical counseling, whether from the pulpit or within a small group or a person-to-person relationship. All ministries are important in growth and change, and counseling is a part of all ministries. As people are led into a closer experience with God, they are more able to meet the problems of living and the challenges of life.

Biblical counseling is not a separate structure attached to the building of believers, but rather a means by which God has chosen to heal and develop His sons and daughters. God's creative molding of each believer is more complex and intricate than the human mind can imagine. However, in this creative process of making believers into the image of Christ, God uses human vessels and human means along with His divine means. When a church is providing counsel from the pulpit, from the small group, and from personal relationships, people know where to turn when they are facing difficult situations and changes in their lives.

3

Model of Man

Conversation is the most prominent activity in counseling. Words are used and exchanged, problems and feelings described, understanding sought, advice or suggestions given and sometimes received. Elliott Evans, addressing a conference sponsored by the National Council of Teachers of English, complained about a "gradual debasement of the language" and told the teachers that "the use of language is a moral act."[1] Jesus said, "Not what enters into the mouth defiles the man, but what proceeds out of the mouth, this defiles the man" (Matthew 15:11). Just as a ship has a small rudder to steer its course, so too in counseling: conversation is of great consequence. Although actual change depends on the counselee, the *direction* of that change is encouraged through conversation.

Behind the dominant feature of conversation, there is a model of man, which every counselor has, and a methodology, which every counselor uses. The model tells *why* people behave the way they do, and the methodology tells *how* to accomplish change. In the next two chapters we will discuss the rationale (model of man) and in chapters 5 and 6 the ritual (methodology) that encourages change. The *why* of human behavior and the *how* to change it are already contained in Scripture. Therefore it is unnecessary to turn to any psychological system.

1. Elliott Evans, quoted by Bob English, "Language Is a Moral Act," *University of California Clip Sheet* 58, no. 9 (28 April 1981).

THE PSYCHOLOGICAL MODEL

Each approach to counseling is based upon some model of man, which includes a description of personality and an explanation of behavior. A psychological model of man may be elaborate in that it describes the basic nature, growth stages, aberrant behavior, and normal behavior, analyzed and categorized with great detail. Some of these models, such as Freud's psychoanalytic model, have been created through the observation of a limited number of atypical individuals. Few systems have been developed after observing a relatively normal segment of the population. Although observations of behavior may be somewhat objective, explanations for behavior are generally subjective. Therefore, every man-made model is a subjective interpretation of man and his behavior. Because it is presented in scientific-sounding language, a psychological model will generally appear more objective and accurate than it really is.

In an article titled "Theory as Self-Portrait and the Ideal of Objectivity" psychologist Linda Riebel points out clearly that "theories of human nature reflect the theorist's personality as he or she externalizes it or projects it onto humanity at large." She says, "The theory of human nature is a self-portrait of the theorist . . . emphasizing what the theorist needs." Her main point is that the theorizing in psychotherapy "cannot transcend the individual personality engaged in that act."[2] Psychologist Charles Tart accuses psychology of being "culture bound."[3]

The psychological way presents various models of man and different methods of understanding him. There are four major models of psychotherapy. The first two, psychoanalytic and behavioristic, rose out of a technological society that attempted to reduce everything to a machine in order to understand it. These two psychological models present a mechanical view of man in which he is either determined by his early psychosexual stages of development (psychoanalytic) or by his environment (behavioristic). Either way man is looked at and treated as a lock-step organism.

The other two basic models, humanistic and existential, moved away from determinism. According to the humanistic model, individuals are not responsible for who they are, but they have free will

2. Linda Riebel, "Theory as Self-Portrait and the Ideal of Objectivity," *Journal of Humanistic Psychology* 22, no. 2 (Spring 1982): 91-92.
3. Charles Tart, *Transpersonal Psychologies* (New York: Harper & Row, 1975), p. 4.

and can choose to change. Self is the central focus. The human is elevated to godhood because self, apart from God, has all the answers to life's problems. After first describing man as a machine and then as autonomous and godlike, psychology has recently contrived a fourth model of man, which is the existential, or transpersonal. Whereas psychotherapy arose as an alternative to religion and even criticized man's religious outlook (Freud), the existential or transpersonal psychological model not only admits man's spiritual needs, but uses forms of spiritual experience as means of psychological relief. The model provides remedies to the problems of living through spiritual means by looking to Eastern religions and by including elements of the occult.

It is strange that psychotherapy, which arose as a denial of religious answers to the problems of living, has now returned to the spiritual realm. But rather than presenting the good news of Jesus Christ, this religious psychotherapy offers any number of false religious and mystical practices as solutions to the trials and tribulations of life. Instead of looking to the one true and living God, many are running after the myths of men and worshiping the idols of men's minds within the psychotherapeutic setting.

Under each of these four basic models there are various other models, each differing somewhat from the next. Some of these models are seemingly biblical. For example, some psychotherapies emphasize love. Carl Rogers, the best-known and most admired humanistic psychologist, says that his crowning discovery from a lifetime of counseling is that of love. But his kind of love excludes God, who is the source of all true love. Therefore, although certain similarities exist between a biblical model and a psychological model, it is better to rely upon the Word of God and the work of the Holy Spirit than upon the opinions of men.

Psychological models basically distort the gospel, and some are light-years away from the truth. For example, Freud described man's mind in terms of id, ego, and superego. These bear a strong resemblance to body, soul, and spirit, respectively. Such a description does not add to Scripture but supplants it with distortion and with unbiblical explanations of personhood. Quite often individual therapists will brew up a new model with a will from Glasser, an unconscious from Freud, a body from Skinner, and a scream from Janov. Furthermore, once a therapist has concocted his own brew, he may change the recipe from time to time. Nevertheless, the model to which a counselor subscribes will influence the entire course of counseling.

VALUES

Within the framework of the model of man there is a world view with a set of values. How a person views life and perceives certain values influences his life and behavior. Therefore, it is extremely important for the counselor and the counselee to share the same basic view of man and the same values. The counselee needs to be aware at least of the counselor's view of life and his values so that he can decide if the counselor is someone with whom he wants to work. It may be that the counselee would like to adopt the same views and values as the counselor. In that case there would be no conflict. If there is conflict or confusion in this area, however, the counselee should find another counselor.

A counselor's view of life and his concept of man and the world form a backdrop against which he works. Many writers and researchers admit that one cannot counsel without a value system. Research psychologist Allen Bergin has made the following statements:

Values are an inevitable and pervasive part of psychotherapy.[4]

There is an ideology in everyone's therapy.

Techniques thus become a medium for mediating the value influence intended by the therapist.

A value free approach is impossible.[5]

Bergin also confesses that sometimes the therapist or counselor assumes that what he does "is professional without recognizing that [he is] purveying under the guise of professionalism and science [his] own personal value [system]."[6] Elsewhere he says, "It will not do for

---

4. Allen Bergin, "Psychotherapy and Religious Values," *Journal of Consulting and Clinical Psychology* 48, no. 1 (1980): 97.

5. Allen Bergin, "Psychotherapeutic Change and Humanistic Versus Religious Values," BMA Audio Cassette, #T-301 (New York: Guilford, 1979).

6. Bergin, "Psychotherapy and Religious Values," pp. 101-2.

therapists to hide their prejudices behind a screen of scientific jargon."[7]

Hans Strupp says, "There can be no doubt that the therapist's moral and ethical values are always 'in the picture.' "[8] Perry London believes that avoidance of values is impossible. "Every aspect of psychotherapy presupposes some implicit moral doctrine."[9] Further, "Moral considerations may dictate, in large part, how the therapist defines his client's needs, how he operates in the therapeutic situation, how he defines 'treatment,' and 'cure,' and even 'reality.' "[10] Morse and Watson conclude, "Thus values and moral judgments will always play a role in therapy, no matter how much the therapist attempts to push them to the background."[11]

Carl Rogers, in his nondirective therapy, claims that he does not influence the client in any way. Because the person expresses himself in any way he chooses, many believe nondirective therapy is value-free. However, Jay Haley says:

> Actually nondirective therapy is a misnomer. To state that any communication between two people can be nondirective is to state an impossibility.[12]

Without intending to do so, a counselor will communicate some response and thus influence the client's thoughts, words, and actions.[13] Two independent studies done ten years apart showed that Rogers himself was, in fact, a directive counselor.[14] His response to his clients rewarded and punished and therefore reinforced or extinguished certain expressions of the clients. If Carl Rogers cannot be nondirective, it is certainly unlikely that any other psychothera-

---

7. Bergin, "Behavior Therapy," p. 11.
8. Hans Strupp, "Some Observations on the Fallacy of Value-free Therapy and the Empty Organism," in *Psychotherapies: A Comparative Casebook,* ed. Steven Morse and Robert Watson (New York: Holt, Rinehart, and Winston, 1977), p. 313.
9. Perry London, *The Modes and Morals of Psychotherapy* (New York: Holt, Rinehart, and Winston, 1964), pp. 1-40, 6.
10. Ibid. p. 5.
11. Steven Morse and Robert Watson, *Psychotherapies: A Comparative Casebook* (New York: Holt, Rinehart, and Winston, 1977), p. 3.
12. Jay Haley, *Strategies of Psychotherapy* (New York: Grune and Stratton, 1963), p. 71.
13. Ibid., p. 82.
14. E. J. Murray, "A Content-analysis Method for Studying Psychotherapy," *Psychological Monographs* 70 (13, Whole no. 420), 1956. C. B. Truax, "Reinforcement and Nonreinforcement in Rogerian Psychotherapy," *Journal of Abnormal Psychology* 71 (1966): 1-9.

pist or counselor can refrain from being directive in one way or another. Thus, values will seep through any system and influence a counselee.

Some behavior therapists claim to provide value-free psychotherapy. They claim to modify behavior through certain manipulative means which can be divorced from the values of the therapist. (If there are no values, one wonders why there needs to be a change in behavior in the first place.) Strupp describes a case of a man whose goal for counseling was to change from pedophilia (sexual attraction to young boys) to homosexuality directed toward adult men. He noted that since the therapist was willing to work toward this goal, the therapist's value system condoned homosexuality; otherwise he would be going against his own values. Strupp concludes his discussion by saying that "the therapist is a powerful moral force and that value-free therapy is a fiction."[15]

Allen Bergin recommends that therapists publicize where they stand concerning values and morals. He says that it is appropriate for a therapist to offer the client a brochure indicating his value orientation. He also believes that a therapist should state his personal values at critical points in therapy.[16] For example, if the subject of premarital or extramarital sex comes up, the therapist should at least declare where he stands. This is rarely (if ever) done in psychotherapy, but we concur with Bergin and even believe that the law should require each counselor to hand a value statement to each counselee before counseling begins. Such a statement could curtail business, however, since there is often a difference between the value systems of therapist and client.

A study of religious practices and convictions of psychiatrists and related professions, including psychologists and social workers, indicates a low percentage of church/temple affiliation and a moderately low percentage of overall religiosity.[17] The averages for the total population swing the other direction.[18] Therefore, there is often bound to be some dichotomy between the values of the counselor and the counselee in psychotherapy.

15. Strupp, pp. 312-15.
16. Allen Bergin, personal interview, January 15, 1980.
17. William E. Henry et al., The Fifth Profession (San Francisco: Jossey-Bass, 1971), pp. 68-69.
18. "The Christianity Today—Gallup Poll: An Overview," Christianity Today, 21 December 1979, pp. 12-15.

The counselor will be more effective and the counselee will have a greater opportunity for improving if both have similar values. Imagine a man who believes in open marriage, has no respect for the family or family life, and thinks God is dead coming to a biblical counselor for help. It would be a wonderful opportunity for evangelism, but the value system, rather than the goals of the counselee, would be the focus. Conversely, imagine a Christian's going to a secular counselor who has the same value orientation as the first man mentioned. The subtle and direct influence of such a counselor would demean, if not destroy, the religious values of the Christian. Research shows that just such discrepancies often exist.[19]

Values of psychotherapy have subverted those of Christianity. Torrey notes the transition from one influence to another:

> As religious influence has died, however, there has been a search for a new set of absolutes. Psychiatry has been willing to sanctify its values with the holy water of medicine and offer them up as the true faith of "Mental Health." It is a false Messiah.[20]

On the other hand, many are despairing of the promises of psychotherapy. Henry Fairly, in his book *The Seven Deadly Sins Today*, says:

> I have for a long time thought that the psychological explanations of the waywardness of our own behavior and the sociological explanations of the evils of our societies have come very nearly to a dead end.[21]

The values the biblical counselor uses have not come to a dead end, however. The Bible explains fully both the waywardness of men and the evils of society.

The spiritual counselor needs to declare that the source of all values and truth is the Bible and that he will rely on the Word of God as the standard in all situations. The Word of God must be both the least and the greatest common denominator for Christians who need counseling and for Christians who give counsel. There is no hidden agenda in biblical counseling as there often is in secular counseling.

19. Bergin, "Psychotherapy and Religious Values," p. 101.
20. E. Fuller Torrey, *The Death of Psychiatry* (Radnor, Pa.: Chilton, 1974), p. 107.
21. Henry Fairlie, *The Seven Deadly Sins Today* (Washington: New Republic, 1978), p. vii.

4

Biblical Model of Man

The Bible describes the human condition and provides understanding about why people behave the way they do. The biblical model of man is based upon the premise that God created mankind to live in relationship with Himself and to reflect His character. He imparted spiritual life as well as physical life so that there might be a profound communion between Creator and creature. But through unbelief, self-will, and pride, man fell from that relationship into a sinful condition from which only Jesus can redeem him.

From a biblical perspective, problems of living lie not only in the realm of the soul, but also in the realm of the spirit. God's purpose is for a person's whole life to emanate from a relationship of love with Him. Biblical solutions to life's problems lie within this spiritual relationship.

Confusion arises when mental-emotional-behavioral problems are dealt with from a psychological rather than, or in addition to, a spiritual perspective. To attempt to combine the biblical truth that mankind is born in sin with a model that says, "Man is intrinsically good" (Rogers), or, "Man begins from a position of I'm Not OK—You're OK" (Harris), or, "Human love and human worthwhileness are man's greatest needs" (Glasser), or any other humanly contrived model, will bring confusion and distortion.

The Bible clearly states that man's condition is fallen until he is redeemed by Jesus to live by the indwelling Holy Spirit in relationship to God the Father. To develop a model of man with explanations such as primal anxiety, need for transcendence, or cosmic loneliness is to avoid the sin question and thereby to miss the only lasting means of restoration: the death and resurrection of Christ. Mankind's condition is not due to the birth process (Otto Rank), nor from early "psychosexual stages of development" (Sigmund Freud), nor from the "primal pool of pain" (Arthur Janov). Nor is it due to any of the other hundreds of guesses and opinions of men about man. Problems of living are basically spiritual because in some way they involve the fallen or redeemed condition of man. And the way to meet those problems is spiritual.

The biblical model of man stands upon three major events: creation, separation, and restoration. God created mankind in His image with free will (choice and responsibility), and in a love relationship with Himself. But man separated himself from God through sin. Because of His great love and because of His original intention for mankind, God provided the means of restoration of relationship. Throughout creation, separation, and restoration, God's love for humanity is the most important fact about mankind.

CREATION

God created humans as spiritual beings with individual uniqueness and with free will. He made individuals in His own image to live in a love relationship with Himself. Within this concept, "in His image," is found God's moral character, His will, and His enablement. "In His image" gives individuals mind, will, and emotion along with the ability, freedom, and opportunity to live according to God's purposes. An essential need is built into mankind: to reflect God in such a way as to obey Him, one must live in relationship to Him. People were not created to live independently from God. Instead, they were created to live in active, cooperative, obedient dependence on God, who is the source of life, love, truth, strength, and character.

Because of Adam and Eve's involvement in the purposes of God for them   to have children and to rule over the earth—there had to be a relationship of love, trust, and oneness of purpose. God provided Adam and Eve with a practical choice to obey Him and thereby live in relationship to Him in oneness of purpose.

> And the Lord God commanded the man, saying, "From any tree of the garden you may eat freely; but from the tree of the knowledge of good and evil you shall not eat, for in the day that you eat from it you shall surely die." (Genesis 2:16-17)

The tree represented a life of independent choice based on one's own values and desires rather than on the will of God. God's commandment implied free will and moral responsibility. It provided an opportunity to reflect his truth and righteousness. As long as Adam and Eve lived in a dependent relationship with God and as long as they reflected Him, they would be willing to limit themselves to obedience.

SEPARATION

If one does not believe God's Word or trust in His love, he sins and separates himself from the very source of life and love. The progression of sin is clearly outlined in the first temptation (Genesis 3). The Word of God is attacked and the love of God violated. Temptations follow the enticements of Satan's words in the Garden as he questions and contradicts God's Word. Satan's words strike at the very root of the love relationship between God and His children. They strike at faith in God by undermining His Word; they strike at hope in God by directing it toward self; and they strike at love by replacing God's love with self-love.

The same temptations that were in the Garden continue this day to keep individuals from coming into relationship with God or to prevent the children of God from living the new life in relationship with God. This is Satan's plan: to separate mankind from God so that he can gain control. Since humans were created to live in relationship to God, they live in a desperately distorted condition—sin—until they are reunited to God and learn to live His way. Thus a biblical counselor will always seek to bring a counselee into a closer relationship with God through faith, hope, and love.

FAITH UNDERMINED

The very authenticity of God's Word and the trustworthiness of His character are wrapped up in Satan's initial question: "Indeed, has God said?" Through this fateful conversation, the Word of God was undermined through several techniques of which Christian counselors and counselees need to be aware: questioning, altering, embellishing, distorting, contradicting, discrediting, forsaking, and ignoring God's Word.

In even considering the possibility that perhaps God had *not* said, Eve's hold on the truth loosened just enough for Satan to thrust forth a direct contradiction: "You surely shall not die." Then he deviously discredited God and His Word, making it appear evil: "For God knows that in the day you eat from it your eyes will be opened, and you will be like God, knowing good and evil" (Genesis 3:5). This statement was loaded with insinuations and distortions. Eve was now ready to believe the lie: to forsake the truth and follow the word of Satan. Once she forsook God's Word, she was able to ignore it, look at the forbidden fruit, and decide for herself whether it was good or evil.

If one does not believe that all of God's commands proceed from His love, he will walk in the deception of his own ideas and imaginations. If one does not believe the wisdom of God's commands and the truth of consequences related to disobedience, he enters into the shadow of deceit and begins to live a lie. Faith is supplanted by doubt, and truth is rejected. Only by trusting God's love as expressed through His Word, through His Son, and through His Holy Spirit can one avoid the pitfalls of sin.

Once a person doubts God's Word and thus His very character, he has moved out of the protective place of relationship. In undermining faith in God and belief in His Word, Satan makes one vulnerable to further temptation. A Christian must live by "every word that proceeds out of the mouth of God" (Matthew 4:4).

Although the original temptation of Eve may seem remote from our lives today, this temptation to doubt God's word and character is a powerful potential problem not only underlying many problems of living but preventing people from solving such problems. God has given us His Word in the Bible. Will we believe the Word, or will we doubt it—or worse yet, disbelieve it and ignore it? This is not a simple question. Many churchgoers may say that they believe the Bible, but their lives do not demonstrate that faith. Others readily admit that they doubt what they have not experienced to be true.

The Bible speaks of the sinfulness of man and the sacrifice of Christ. Do we really believe that we are sinners? Do we really believe that "all our righteousnesses are as filthy rags in the sight of God"? Do we really believe that "all have sinned and come short of the glory of God"? Or did we come to Jesus with some residue of goodness or some sense of merit? Has Jesus paid the perfect price for our sins? Is His blood sufficient to cover all past, present, and future sins?

Although these questions seem almost catechismal in their tone, they are monumental in their meaning. We constantly find individuals who do not believe a variety of biblical doctrines or cannot apply them to their own lives. In truth this is a constant struggle in small or great measure for all believers, but it is often a critical problem for those facing life's difficulties, because it is at those times that our beliefs are challenged and we are pressed to see if we really believe what God has said.

As one is counseling, this tension between belief and disbelief must be explored, examined, and remedied if necessary. Satan's ploy needs to be explained and guarded against. Some forms of contradictions are quite subtle and yet visible if the counselor keeps the Word of God fresh in his own life. Such statements as "God doesn't forgive me," or "How can God expect me to forgive my husband?" or "I'm really a good person," all contain subtle, yet obvious, contradictions to God's Word.

HOPE MISDIRECTED

Hope is that aspect of faith which looks to the future. God had given Adam and Eve hope for continued relationship, for family, and for purpose in life. Their hope lay in their relationship to God. Satan gave them a false hope through the lie, "You surely shall not die," and through the deceptive promise, "You will be like God, knowing good and evil."

Whereas God created mankind to hope in Him, false hope centers in self, denies the consequences of sin, and leads to despair. Three facets of false hope often come into play during counseling. One has to do with immortality, the second with escaping the consequences of behavior, and the third with self-sufficiency.

The feeling of *immortality* is almost instinctive in our culture. Death is hidden away and relegated to obscure corners of life so that people will not be constantly confronted with it. Although newspapers are filled with death, individuals rarely conceive of or cope with the concept of personal death. Recently, there has even been a rise of the false hope of immortality through reincarnation and through so-called death experiences which deny both death and judgment.

In our youth and pleasure-oriented society we have focused on life and enjoyment rather than on death and self-sacrifice. If a man could see the preeminence of death and know the fine line between death and life, he would no doubt have a greater respect for his family, friends, church, work, and particularly his relationship to God. Many people sin as if there were no tomorrow. As people pour out their troubles it is good to examine their view of life and death.

Satan's statements promise that man can *escape the consequences* of disobeying God. Such false hope eliminates the need for responsibility. After Adam and Eve ate of the "tree of the knowledge of good and evil," God entered the Garden and questioned Adam. Adam immediately blamed "the woman," and Eve immediately blamed "the serpent." The pattern they began of unbelief that leads to irresponsibility, which quickly turns to blame, is also prominent today.

The false hope of *self-sufficiency* is the hallmark of secular humanism, which places man as the final judge of right and wrong, the obvious fruit of the tree of the knowledge of good and evil. Humanism elevates the human mind and emotion to the place God should hold and places the hope for mankind in man. Self-sufficiency breeds self-glorification, but it also leads to self-condemnation and man-made religions of self-effort. False hope in self may lead to temporary glory, but it finally ends in despair as evidenced in godless forms of existentialism.

LOVE DISTORTED

Man violated God's love and ruptured his relationship with God by believing Satan's promise, "You will be like God." This temptation is central to man's Fall, and overcoming it is crucial to his restoration and growth. Problems of living must be viewed through the struggle between God's love and self-love and between God's lordship and self's lordship.

In discrediting God's Word, Satan denied God's love. In essence, he was saying to Eve, "God knows that the day you eat from it wonderful things will happen to you." He implied that God was withholding good from Eve because He did not really love her. That was just enough for Eve to look to herself for good. As soon as she moved away from believing God's love she turned to herself and to self-love. If God were not going to give her what she considered best, she would take it for herself.

As soon as Eve doubted God's love, she became her own god, deciding what was good and what was evil. And, as she "saw that the tree was *good* for food, and that it was a *delight* to the eyes, and that the tree was *desirable* to make one wise, she took from its fruit and ate; and she gave also to her husband with her, and he ate" (Genesis 3:6; emphasis added). When human reason and desire replace God's Word and God's love, the person easily moves into sin and draws others along. Sin is both the cause and result of separation from God.

Sin is definitely a love problem. John warned:

> Do not love the world, nor the things in the world. If anyone loves the world, the love of the Father is not in him. For all that is in the world, the lust of the flesh and the lust of the eyes and the boastful pride of life, is not from the Father, but is from the world. (1 John 2:15-16)

When love for God is diminished through personal desires, lust replaces love and a person sets himself up for a great range of wrong thoughts, motivations, emotions, attitudes, and actions.

> But each one is tempted when he is carried away and enticed by his own lust. Then when lust has conceived, it gives birth to sin; and when sin is accomplished, it brings forth death. (James 1:14-15)

Adam and Eve followed a lie instead of truth, turned love into selfish desire, and trusted the liar instead of God. Their independent, sinful self was formed out of the fruit of the knowledge of good and evil, their relationships became distorted and self-serving, their purpose was twisted to be gods themselves, and their will came under the influence of evil.

The Bible shows the vulnerabilities and struggles of humanity. The vulnerabilities exist either in the Adamic nature (fallen man) or in the flesh of redeemed man. These appear in a variety of forms, such as pride, self-will, and rebellion, which are all expressions of self-love. Joined with the vulnerabilities are struggles such as pride versus humility, self-will versus obedience, and rebellion versus submission. These struggles between self-love and God's love are central in the battle between the flesh and the Spirit and in the battle between wanting "my way" and submitting to His will. The primary tension of humanity lies between believing God or believing a lie, between hoping in God or hoping in self, and between living in a love relationship with God or loving oneself more than God and others.

God created individuals to live under His loving rule. But natural humanity is under a form of self-rule influenced by Satan (Ephesians 2:1-3). Because of the inherited sin nature, our natural selves are not adequate to rule without distortion and self-centeredness. Thus those who are not living in submission to God end up being ruled by their own feelings, faulty reasoning, reactions to circumstances, and pressures from significant persons in their environment. They attempt to meet personal needs and desires through self-effort and/or manipulation of the environment and other people. And they try to protect themselves through self-defense, self-justification, and casting blame.

Although such persons may admit that there is a higher power and even strive for some standard of morality, they are separated from the God who created them until they receive new life through Christ by faith and live according to His life within them by faith. Until they are rightly related to God, they have an inaccurate view of God and of themselves. From such a position it is very easy to develop problems of living and severe problems of rejection, rebellion, resentment, bitterness, unforgiveness, depression, anxiety, purposelessness, and a distorted conception of God, self, and others. All these stem from the sin nature, which is the self not yielded to God.

Most contemporary psychological theories contend that people are essentially good and that society is the culprit. The Bible, on the other hand, reveals the lost and sinful condition of mankind. As long as a person is separated from the nature of God and the identity of God, he is limited in his ability to choose the right way.

> For the mind set on the flesh is death, but the mind set on the Spirit is life and peace; because the mind set on the flesh is hostile toward God; for it does not subject itself to the Law of God, for it is not even able to do so; and those who are in the flesh cannot please God. (Romans 8:6-8)

Apart from God, man fails in moral responsibility.

RESTORATION

Because of His great love, God provided salvation from separation. Shortly after Adam and Eve separated themselves from God, He promised a redeemer who would reconcile sinners (those separated from God) to relationship with Himself. The entire Old Testament reveals ways through which God enabled mankind to live in relation to Himself and to live in moral responsibility. But all of those ways were temporary and were a foreshadow of Jesus Christ (Hebrews 10:1, 10).

Through His life, death, and resurrection, Jesus demonstrated the love of God, paid the penalty for sin, and provided the permanent means for people to be brought back into relationship with God. All biblical counseling is based upon the redemption of man through the cross of Christ. Those who believe on the name of Jesus and therefore turn from their sins become children of God (John 1:12). As children of God, believers are able to draw near to Him and receive mercy and grace. At spiritual rebirth (John 3:3, 6-7), believers are given the Holy Spirit to dwell within them to guide them and to enable them to obey God's will (Romans 8:9; Galatians 4:4-6). And through the Bible God reveals what they need to know to live according to His plan. From this place of restoration comes relationship and the enabling to live as God created them to live.

When a person becomes a believer he receives new life. He is a new creation in Christ. From this point he begins to mature through facing problems God's way instead of the old way. He is not suddenly translated out of this world of everyday problems, but he has been given a new life which will have opportunities to grow through the challenges of life. He may now choose between living according to the old ways or according to the Word of God.

The themes of creation and separation describe the condition of humanity. Restoration focuses on relationship, new life, and continued transformation. We will discuss these topics further in chapter 6.

BIBLICAL STANDARD FOR LIVING

Scripture provides the only purely accurate description of humanity and principles for change. As one seeks to understand man, he may study psychology or sociology, he may read great literature that looks into the very heart of man, and he may observe human nature for himself. But the only information to use from outside sources is that which survives the scrutiny of Scripture. The Bible, not pragmatism, is the standard.

Besides giving an accurate picture of mankind and a true revelation of God, the Bible presents a living demonstration of mental-emotional soundness. The standard for living in the Bible is not found by looking at the so-called average person, nor is it merely the absence of symptoms. The delineation of mental-emotional maturity is Jesus Christ Himself. He is the only person who lived without the contamination of sin. He is the only person who has met the biblical purpose and standard of personhood: to reflect God and to live in relationship to Him. Jesus is the only person to perfectly reflect the Father's character with thoughts and behavior consistent with mercy and truth. Jesus not only demonstrated how to live; He revealed the character of God, and He provided the means for mankind to change from the fallen condition to the new condition of living according to God's plans and purposes. Jesus is the standard and He is the way.

In addition, the Bible answers the ultimate questions about life. The Bible not only tells about the past, present, and future of man, but it provides meaning in life. When university students were asked, "What do you think is the most crucial question facing young adults today?" 90 percent answered, "What is the meaning of life?"[1] If a person has no purpose and life has no meaning, why take responsibility, why change, and why live? The biblical counselor has confidence in this most important area because he has answers the world cannot give, answers for the cry of the human heart to know the origins, purpose, and destiny of mankind. The biblical counselor's constant frame of reference is the God of the Bible and His Word, which contains principles, practices, and power for living according to divine purposes. A psychotherapist, on the other hand, often dwells on the past, but has nothing to say about the origin, purpose, or destiny of mankind.

The biblical model is complete in that it presents an accurate description of man, a true revelation of why he behaves the way he does, and a perfect standard for living. Moreover, the biblical model presents man from God's perspective and in relationship to Him.

---

1. Ronald Cottle, "Finding Direction for Your Life in 1981," *The Pentecostal Evangel*, 4 January 1981, p. 3.

The Bible shows God's love through creation, man's sinful separation, and God's provision of restoration.

The direction of counseling and the truth of the conversation are imperative in spiritual counseling. Although change may occur whether one is a psychological counselor or a biblical counselor, the model of man with its value system must be scriptural for change to be in the proper direction. What is the sense of change, or even relief for that matter, if it does not conform to a biblically desirable goal? Because the biblical goal is for every believer to be conformed to the image of Christ (Romans 8:29), all spiritual counseling must be heading in that direction. Just as Paul said that he travailed until "Christ be formed" in the early Christians, so too, the biblical counselor works toward this same goal.

5

Methodology for Change

Every counselor uses some methodology to achieve change. *The Psychotherapy Handbook* advertises itself as "The A to Z guide to more than 250 different therapies in use today."[1] These methodologies have yet to show themselves superior to each other, and there is a great deal of confusion and conflict between the various approaches. It appears that any practice that involves a promise in the hands of a practitioner with personality will produce some results.

THE KEYS TO BRINGING ABOUT CHANGE

Methodologies include numerous techniques to motivate counselees and to implement change. Yet, as we will discuss in later chapters, the most important elements in change lie in the human factors: the counselee and the counselor. Therefore, no matter what techniques are used, if a counselee does not want to change, there will be no change. If a counselee truly desires to change and the counselor possesses certain interpersonal qualities, there will be change—no matter what methodology is used.

Given groups of counselees who are equally motivated to change, the results of different types of counseling will be about the same, almost regardless of method. This is probably why it has been

1. Richie Herink, ed., *The Psychotherapy Handbook* (New York: New American Library, 1980).

stated that "all psychotherapies work equally well."[2] After reviewing an enormous amount of research, Mary Smith and her colleagues concluded, "Different types of psychotherapy (verbal or behavioral; psychodynamic, client-centered, or systematic desensitization) do not produce different types or degrees of benefit."[3] Therefore, as important as the methodology is to the *direction* of change, whether or not change occurs depends more upon the counselee than the method. Even the *Handbook of Psychotherapy and Behavior Change* indicates that the counselee is the most important factor, with the counselor next and "technique variables coming in a distant third."[4]

SYSTEMS USED BY CHRISTIAN PSYCHOTHERAPISTS

To determine methodological systems used by Christians who practice psychotherapy, we conducted a survey with the Christian Association for Psychological Studies (CAPS), a national Christian organization composed of numerous practicing therapists. In our survey we used a simple questionnaire in which we asked the psychotherapists to list in order the psychotherapeutic approaches that most influenced their private practices. We listed only ten approaches, but provided blank spaces at the bottom of the sheet for adding others before final ranking. The results indicated that Client-Centered Therapy (Rogers) and Reality Therapy (Glasser) were the two top choices, and that psychoanalysis (Freud) and Rational Emotive Therapy (Ellis) followed closely behind. Nouthetic Counseling (Jay Adams), the only biblical approach listed, tied for last place.

One especially interesting result from the survey is that many of the psychotherapists listed a variety of approaches at the end of the form as well as checking and ranking many of the approaches listed. Their doing so indicates that they have a highly eclectic approach to counseling. In our conclusion we had this to say:

> If this survey constitutes a representative sample, it is probably fair to say that there is not just one Christian psychotherapeutic way. There is

2. "Ambiguity Pervades Research on Effectiveness of Psychotherapy," *Brain/Mind* 7, no. 16 (4 October 1982): 2.
3. Mary Smith, Gene Glass, and Thomas Miller, *The Benefits of Psychotherapy* (Baltimore: Johns Hopkins U., 1980), p. 184.
4. Allen Bergin and Michael Lambert, "The Evaluation of Therapeutic Outcomes," in *Handbook of Psychotherapy and Behavior Change*, ed. Sol Garfield and Allen Bergin, 2d ed. (New York: John Wiley & Sons, 1978), p. 180.

a great variety in the approaches influencing the clinical practices of CAPS members. This survey seems to demonstrate that, while some psychotherapies are more influential than others in the practice of Christian counseling, in general the Christian psychotherapist is both independent and eclectic in his approach to counseling.[5]

Each Christian practicing psychotherapy has his own conglomeration of approaches. That is not surprising. Parloff observes, "Most psychotherapists are eclectic either by intent or default."[6]

Why should the church refer members to the myriad of methods in psychotherapy when no one has shown that any one or combination of these ways is any better than the variety of ways that arise from Scripture? Since there is such disparity between the psychotherapies and since any form of therapy a person devises appears to work, it seems that scriptural methods would be at least as effective as any form of psychotherapy. Therefore, we see no point in combining the methodologies of secular psychotherapies with that of Scripture. And whenever there is a similarity, there is no point in giving credit to the secular therapist who "discovered" a truth that was in Scripture long before he was born.

TRANSCENDENTAL MEDITATION

In chapter 3 we mentioned the four psychological models (psychoanalytic, behavioristic, humanistic, and existential) out of which come four psychotherapeutic approaches, and we noted that the fourth, the existential or transpersonal, which is itself religious and spiritual, includes Eastern religions rather than Christianity and thus implies reliance upon new gods. Daniel Goleman, in a presentation titled "The Reception of Eastern Psychologies in the West," indicates that most Eastern religions "have at their core an esoteric psychology." Goleman speaks of the Eastern path to transformation and concludes, "Finally, all the Eastern psychologies agree that the main means to this transformation of self is meditation."[7]

5. Martin Bobgan and Deidre Bobgan, "Psychotherapeutic Methods of CAPS Members," *Christian Association for Psychological Studies Bulletin* 6, no. 1 (1980): 13.
6. Morris Parloff, "Psychotherapy and Research: An Anaclitic Depression," *Psychiatry* 43 (November 1980): 291.
7. Daniel Goleman, "The Reception of Eastern Psychologies in the West" (Dialogue Discussion Paper; Santa Barbara: Center for the Study of Democratic Institutions, 5 June 1978).

Of all the Eastern meditative approaches to mental and physical change, the best known is transcendental meditation (trademarked TM). TM, which has almost two million practitioners worldwide, is a simple meditative technique that can be learned in a brief period of time and then practiced fifteen to twenty minutes twice a day. Proponents of TM cite research to support their claim that all kinds of mental-emotional-behavioral and physical changes occur for its practitioners.

Although many in the secular world and some in the church accept the claims of TM and other transpersonal therapies, few in the church realize that the cure of souls is and has been a successful method of help. The institution of psychological practices in the church and in Christian seminaries is usually applauded, while cries for a restoration of the cure-of-souls ministry are ignored. The church is in awe of the psychological way, but rejects the biblical way.

NEED FOR THE CURE-OF-SOULS MINISTRY

Clearly, it is difficult for a psychologized church in the midst of a psychotherapized society to return to the cure-of-souls ministry— but return it must. A pastor from a main-line denominational church confessed, "A member comes to me for counseling. I can counsel any number of therapies, but the real question is: How do I help her to grow spiritually? We are not trained for that."[8] There is an answer to the problem he describes. In both model and methodology the psychoanalytic, behavioristic, humanistic, and existential approaches are not only unproved but unnecessary. The most powerful way to minister to the hurts of humanity is the biblical way. If a counselee is desirous of change, love that contains both mercy and truth will prevail over problems and will motivate a counselee to change.

EFFICACY OF NONPSYCHOLOGICAL MODELS

People have wondered if it is possible to minister to mental-emotional-behavioral problems without resorting to psychological models and methods or to psychological gimmicks and devices. The evidence suggests that it is. Three researchers found in a national

8. Office for Church Life and Leadership, *Spiritual Development and Christian Community* (New York: United Church of Christ, 1978) p. 3.

survey conducted for the Joint Commission on Mental Illness and Health that "of those persons who actively sought help for personal problems, the vast majority contacted persons other than mental health professionals, and that generally they were more satisfied with the help received than were those who chose psychiatrists and psychologists."[9]

Moreover, individuals can overcome all sorts of problems either on their own or with the help of family and friends. In reporting on the success of therapy programs for individuals who wished to stop smoking and those who wished to reduce their weight, Columbia University professor Stanley Schachter says, "The rates of successful self-cure of cigarette smoking and of obesity are considerably higher than any yet reported in the literature on curing these problems through various therapy programs." In comparing those who quit smoking on their own with those who quit through therapy, Schachter observes, "Those who attempted to quit on their own were at least two to three times more successful than were people in other studies who went for professional help."[10]

Stanton Peele, a top addiction researcher, says, "Among people in therapy to lose weight, stop smoking, kick a drug or drink addiction, as few as 5% actually make it."[11] Peele believes that "therapy itself may inadvertently impede cure."[12] Peele summarizes by saying, "But here's the irony and the hope: Self-cure can work, and depending on someone else to cure you usually does not."[13]

We believe there is some justification to conclude that for all problems of living the best way out is by individual effort; the next best help is the informal support group; then the formal support group; and finally least effective is individual therapy. This is one reason that, in addition to individual biblical counseling, we strongly recommend to our counselees attendance at the regular services of our church and involvement in the loving environment of a small home group.

Training and techniques and education and degrees will always pale in comparison to the motivation of the counselee to change and

9. Bergin and Lambert, p. 149.
10. Stanley Schachter, "Don't Sell Habit-Breakers Short," *Psychology Today*, August 1982, pp. 28-29.
11. Stanton Peele, "Out of the Habit Trap," *American Health*, September/October 1983, p. 42.
12. Ibid., p. 47.
13. Ibid., p. 42.

the encouragement to do so in a loving environment. This one idea will probably be most difficult to comprehend because of the horror stories propagated by psychotherapeutic propaganda about people who have been maltreated by some well-intentioned, but ill-informed, lay person. It is our opinion that the horror stories having to do with professional psychotherapists would overwhelm those told about lay counselors. A history of horror could be told about maltreatment and costly mistakes made by psychotherapists since the beginning of professional psychotherapy.[14] Psychiatrist Thomas Szasz warns that "perhaps most, so-called psychotherapeutic procedures are harmful for the so-called patients . . . and that all such interventions and proposals should therefore be regarded as evil until proven otherwise."[15]

Change can and does occur in both psychological and biblical counseling because of the counselee's motivation and because of the interpersonal qualities of the counselor. Comparison of methodologies does not indicate the superiority of one system of techniques over another. Therefore, why not use biblical counseling, which conforms to Scripture, rather than psychotherapeutic systems, which arise out of the wisdom of men and often conflict with the Word of God?

14. Martin Bobgan and Deidre Bobgan, *The Psychological Way/The Spiritual Way* (Minneapolis: Bethany Fellowship, 1979), pp. 38-41.
15. Thomas Szasz, *The Myth of Psychotherapy* (Garden City, N.Y.: Doubleday, Anchor, 1978), p. xxiii.

6

Biblical Methodology for Change

Biblical methodology for change is actually a spiritual process which operates according to what God has done and according to the individual's faith in God. God has provided all that is necessary for spiritual transformation through His Son, His Holy Spirit, and His Word. Although God accomplishes the change, a person must respond in faith not only for initial salvation and new life, but also for continued sanctification. For counseling to be spiritual, such change must be accomplished by faith, which leads to loving and obeying God.

Biblical counseling involves at least three persons: God, the person seeking help, and one or more Christians who come alongside to minister God's mercy and truth. Because the most vital changes come through the love of God and the person's response, the counselor's primary function is to express the love of God and encourage the person to draw closer to God through faith in His love, which consists of both mercy and truth. An understanding of the biblical model of man gives a basis for evaluating an individual's need and direction for change. The methodology provides an understanding of how God works in a person's life.

The primary principle of biblical counseling is this: As a person moves closer to God through His love—which includes both mercy and truth and is expressed through His Word and through His Holy

Spirit—he will change in the areas of thoughts, emotions, and actions. Five assumptions underlie this basic principle:

1. Initial transformation takes place through faith. When a person becomes a child of God, he becomes a new person indwelt by the Holy Spirit (Romans 8:9-15).

2. Once a person receives new life he is to walk in the Spirit, according to the principles of his new nature, rather than according to the old ways of the self (Galatians 5:22-25).

3. Therefore, the source for meeting all of life's situations is in the spiritual realm—in his relationship to God (2 Peter 1:1-4).

4. Because a Christian is a spiritual being, only the Bible can accurately describe him (model of man, Psalm 94:8-11; Hebrews 4:12-13) and indicate the way to live (methodology of change, Acts 20:32; 1 Thessalonians 2:13).

5. One central biblical doctrine of this spiritual approach is the struggle between God's love and lordship (walking after the Spirit) and the love and lordship of self (walking after the flesh). (See Romans 7:14-25.)

Regardless of the problems experienced, individuals are changed for the better in some way by drawing closer to God through His love. Because we are whole beings, problems of the soul do affect the spirit. Therefore it is unbiblical to treat problems of living as though they are unrelated to the spirit. By biblically dealing with the spiritual implications of the problem, the person will be better able to deal with the mental, emotional, and behavioral aspects. As someone draws close to God, that person is being exposed to both the mercy and truth of God's love. As the person chooses to draw close, God ministers to his spirit so that he finds solutions to his problems.

In an age of technology and sophistication one may overlook the simple biblical fact that bringing a person closer to God through His love will transform life's problems as nothing else can. God's love touches an individual's spirit, and one consistent result of a deepened spiritual life is an improved mental-emotional-behavioral life.

The one common element in both psychological counseling and biblical counseling is that of love. It is the penetrating power of love that softens the ground of the will and encourages the human heart so that change may occur. The change occurs through love, not through psychological techniques and training. The major thesis of Paul Halmos's book *The Faith of the Counsellors* is "that all forms of psychotherapy are based, not on a set of scientific facts or principles, but on an all-pervasive belief in the healing power of love."[1] Even the human love to which Halmos refers has transforming power. But human love can never transform man's spirit; only God's love can do that. God's love is infinitely more intense. God's love is the powerful, consistent, dependable force that, when received, transforms the individual and enables him to walk by faith, to hope in God, and to love God and others according to the Great Commandment (Deuteronomy 6:5; Leviticus 19:18; Matthew 22:36-40).

People have been and will be relieved of every human problem that talk therapy touches through the receiving and giving of God's love. Whatever mental-emotional-behavioral problem will yield to talk therapy will be transformed by love. Everything from simple anxiety to serious alcoholism and from depression to marital difficulties will be best dealt with through God's love. It is this same love that sustained Jesus and the patriarchs and prophets. It is the same love that has, does, and can transform the trials of life.

Problems provide the broken ground into which spiritual seeds of life and love can be planted. A biblical counselor will use the problems of living as a means of bringing a person closer to God. Because moving closer to God is the single most consistent characteristic of those who change, it must be the number one factor in counseling. The counselee and counselor must experience the truth that the greatest obstacle to growth is separation from God and the greatest impetus for growth is moving closer to God and responding to His love. As problems occur our focus is not on the problem, though it is discussed. The focus is on the person and his relationship to God.

As a person encounters problems of living certain tensions and tendencies appear. These are seen in creation, separation, and restoration. Because the biblical events of creation, separation, and restoration are all true, they form a prism through which we can view problems of living and see God's love. Continued application of these facets of the prism will bring transformation of the person and resolution of his problems. The approach requires that a counselor

1. Paul Halmos, *The Faith of the Counsellors* (New York: Schocken, 1970), back cover.

know the Bible well and be able to recognize how these three important historical events affect each individual within his own circumstances.

The counselor and counselee need to consider the following aspects of creation, separation, and restoration:

Creation: 1. Spiritual nature
              2. Uniqueness
              3. Free will and responsibility
Separation: 1. Faith undermined
              2. Hope misdirected
              3. Love distorted
Restoration: 1. Death and resurrection of Christ (new life)
              2. Holy Spirit
              3. Word of God

CREATION

God created humans as spiritual beings to live in relationship with Himself, as unique individuals designed to reflect God, and as persons with free will and responsibility. These three aspects of creation are involved in every situation of life and are therefore present in every problem and resolution.

SPIRITUAL NATURE

Since the nature of humanity is spiritual and since persons were created to live in relationship with God, problems must be viewed as spiritual problems and the resolutions to problems must be seen as found in relationship to God. That is why drawing closer to God is basic to biblical counseling.

UNIQUENESS

No two people are exactly alike, and therefore God will minister to each person individually. The uniqueness of the counselee and the counselor and the way God works differently in each individual's life will result in a unique situation each time two or more people counsel together. In fact, two different Christian counselors may be moved by the Holy Spirit to minister in two different ways to the same individual and yet accomplish the same results.

As one reads about how Jesus ministered to each individual, one learns to depend upon God to lead and learns God's ways of ministering truth in love and power. Not all people received the words of Jesus, and many left Him when they heard more truth than they wanted to hear. But, those who received His words and believed Him were delivered out of darkness and confusion.

FREE WILL AND RESPONSIBILITY

God gave mankind free will. Therefore God does hold persons responsible for thoughts, words, and actions. Ever since the Garden of Eden people have attempted to avoid being responsible. Whenever a person justifies, excuses, or rationalizes his actions, he is attempting to avoid personal responsibility. If a person says he cannot help doing what he does or if he blames another person, he needs to recognize his responsibility and know the Source of his ability to do what is right.

Besides facing the fact that he is responsible for his thoughts, words, and actions, each person is given the choice to change. Even though God ultimately transforms persons, He does so only with the cooperation of the individual. Although God draws him through His love, and although the counselor encourages him to draw close, the counselee is the only one who can make that choice to move closer to God. God has provided the way to draw close through His Son Jesus. Jesus said,

> Come to Me, all who are weary and heavy-laden, and I will give you rest. Take My yoke upon you, and learn from Me, for I am gentle and humble in heart; and you shall find rest for your souls. For My yoke is easy, and My load is light. (Matthew 11:28-30)

The choice to come, to take, to learn, to draw near is the individual's part. Therefore, personal responsibility is an inherent aspect of the biblical methodology of counseling.

SEPARATION

As we discussed in chapter 4, Satan promised Eve, "You will be like God." Christ has redeemed man from the consequences of the Fall through the cross, but the temptation of this one simple promise remains and must be a central consideration in counseling. The original separation from God occurred through unbelief, misdirected hope, and distorted love. People continue to suffer from not believing God, from hoping more in themselves and circumstances than in God, and from loving self more than loving God and neighbor. Even after a person becomes a Christian and receives the life of Jesus within him, he may revert to old ways of thinking and behaving. He may retain certain desires and motivations that are not of God. Therefore, in every counseling situation a person's faith must be examined and encouraged in the direction of God's truth. The person's source of hope must be considered, since false hope ultimately leads to despair. Every counseling conversation should emphasize God's love and encourage love for God.

RESTORATION

God has provided all that is necessary to restore individuals to Himself through the death and resurrection of Christ. Through the cross Jesus saves people from their sinful condition, which has brought separation, and He restores them to new life through His resurrection (Romans 6:4). Thus He has made the way of forgiveness from sin, and He has given people a new life indwelt by the Holy Spirit so that Christians are able to believe God's Word, to hope again in Him, and to love Him with all of their being. Biblical counseling works in this realm of faith, hope, and love. Because of the indwelling Holy Spirit and the availability of God's Word, the biblical counselor and the counselee have all that they need for growth, change, and the resolution of problems.

RESTORATION THROUGH THE DEATH AND RESURRECTION OF CHRIST

The cross of Christ cannot be overemphasized in biblical counseling because Jesus' death paid the price of sin, which separates individuals from God. Thus, to draw close to God, one must go through the cross, which is God's provision for forgiveness, new life, and communion with Him.

1. *Forgiveness.* Sin separates a person from God and prevents him from drawing near. Jesus provided the only remedy for sin through the cross. Because the forgiveness of God cleanses a person from unrighteousness and reestablishes relationship, forgiveness is God's

means of enabling a person to stop sinning. As a person learns to identify his sin by reading and hearing the Word, by looking at Jesus, who lived without sin, and by observing his own actions in the mirror of the Word, he may admit that sin, confess it, and turn from it to look again at Jesus, who is living His righteousness within him through the Holy Spirit. God's forgiveness opens the way into His presence so that believers may draw close to Him to find the wisdom and the enabling that they need to overcome problems.

In dealing with problems of living the believer still has to face the reality of sin because sin is the ultimate source of all such problems. Some problems may not actually be due to a person's own disobedience to God, but all problems do come from living in a sinful world. Problems come from both sinning and being sinned against.

If sin is denied, overlooked, or minimized, it will remain as a constant thorn, aggravating problems of living. Many people fear the thought of facing sin because they do not truly understand the efficacy of the cross of Christ. The walk of a Christian is to be by faith in the shed blood of Jesus so that he may face his sin, confess that it is sin, repent, and be cleansed.

Although some problems may not be caused by personal sin, many are. Even those problems which may seem to have no spiritual connection have a spiritual base. When the enemies came against them, Israel could say that her problems were external and circumstantial. But sin was the root cause, for Israel had turned away from following God. Disobedience to God will result in problems that may seem to have no relationship to specific sin. On the other hand, obeying God in a sinful world will bring its own problems because one is going against the grain of the world. Either way, living in relationship to God will cause one to grow through the problems and find help in the time of need. Whether one sins or is sinned against, Jesus is the answer to the problems of living.

Much secular counseling works from the basis of helping a person have a less severe conscience so that he will not feel guilty. Biblical counseling, on the other hand, will seek to encourage honesty and sensitivity to sin so that repentance and restoration may occur. Rather than getting rid of guilt and self-condemnation through denying sin, learning to forgive oneself, or altering standards, biblical counseling rids one of guilt and condemnation through a reliable standard of justice, through the forgiveness of God, and through repentance and restoration (1 John 1:9). Any form of counseling that does not involve the redemptive work of Jesus and the forgiveness through His blood cannot bring a counselee into the kind of relationship with God whereby he might fulfill the purpose of God: to reflect Him and live in relationship to Him in faith, hope, and love.

2. *New life.* Through identification with the cross, believers become dead to sin and alive to God. "Or do you not know that all of us who have been baptized into Christ Jesus have been baptized into His death?" (Romans 6:3). The old order of life is counted dead through the cross so that the believer may walk in the newness of life through the resurrection.

Jesus broke the power of sin through the cross and opened the way of new life through His resurrection.

> For if we have become united with Him in the likeness of His death, certainly we shall be also in the likeness of His resurrection, knowing this, that our old self was crucified with Him, that our body of sin might be done away with, that we should no longer be slaves to sin. . . . Even so consider yourselves to be dead to sin, but alive to God in Christ Jesus. (Romans 6:5-6, 11)

Because of the resurrection, believers live by faith in Jesus. They have been given new life so that they can walk in the Spirit according to Romans 8. The cross annihilates the old self, and the resurrection establishes the new life.

The death and resurrection of Jesus are not just theological doctrines to understand intellectually. The death and resurrection are basic to the Christian walk. Many believers do not understand the reality of the new life and struggle to live the Christian life through self-effort. Therefore the biblical counselor must continually refer to the cross and the resurrection, for it is at the cross of Christ that the old is discarded and the person may once again live according to the new life.

3. *Communion with God.* Because God is the primary counselor, prayer is a vital aspect of drawing close to Him. Jesus opened the way to the throne of God and sits at the right hand of the Father interceding for us. He is our High Priest who has experienced our humanity and "who has been tempted in all things as we are, yet

without sin" (Hebrews 4:15). We are thus encouraged to "Draw near with confidence to the throne of grace, that we may receive mercy and may find grace to help in time of need" (Hebrews 4:16). Prayer is the privilege of speaking and listening to God and of being heard. Prayer is primarily relationship in communion and it is agreement with God that His will is good and that He will do what is right. True prayer is an expression of faith, hope, and love for God.

RESTORATION AND THE HOLY SPIRIT

After the resurrection Jesus sent His Holy Spirit to indwell believers and thereby strengthen, comfort, sustain, guide, and enable them (John 16:7-14). The presence of the Holy Spirit is the inner resource and power of God as well as the personal presence of God. Jesus knew that Christians could not love God adequately or follow Him sufficiently without His indwelling presence. God loves us so much that His Holy Spirit is there to accomplish transformation of the Christian as he yields himself to God. Thus the biblical methodology of counseling actively involves the presence and participation of the Holy Spirit.

RESTORATION AND THE WORD OF GOD

The Bible is the instruction book for living and is God's inspired word for humanity.

All Scripture is inspired by God and profitable for teaching, for reproof, for correction, for training in righteousness; that the man of God may be adequate, equipped for every good work. (2 Timothy 3:16-17)

God's Word is filled with knowledge, wisdom, and guidance. The Bible reveals God's involvement with individuals. Furthermore, God's Word works powerfully in people.

For the word of God is living and active and sharper than any two-edged sword, and piercing as far as the division of soul and spirit, of both joints and marrow, and able to judge the thoughts and intentions of the heart. (Hebrews 4:12)

Ray Stedman speaks of the Word of God:

> It is complete, there is nothing left out. It is comprehensive, it does
> everything that we need it to do. There is no part of your life, no
> problem that you will ever face in your life, no question with which
> you will ever be troubled, that the Word of God does not speak to and
> illuminate and meet.[2]

Jay Adams says, "The Bible . . . deals with the same issues that all
counseling does." He contends that the Bible should be the "basis for
a Christian's counseling because of what counseling is all about
(changing lives by changing values, beliefs, relationships, attitudes,
behavior)."[3]

The Bible is the only unchanging touchstone to measure
thinking, feeling, and behaving. The Word of God abounds with
guidance and direction for living. Therefore, the methodology of
biblical counseling relies on the Word of God rather than upon the
wisdom of men.

The most outstanding example of faith in God's Word and
reliance on it in the midst of temptation is Jesus' use of the Word in
the Wilderness, where He met the same basic temptations to which
Adam and Eve succumbed in the Garden (Matthew 4:1-17). Because
Jesus trusted God's love and believed His Word, He was able to
resist the temptation.

In all of the temptations, Satan tried to cause Jesus to do
something for Himself rather than obey God and trust Him. He
tempted Him to look out for "number one," rather than to love and
obey the Father. His ploy is "Take care of yourself; be good to
yourself," with the implication that no one else will. We are living in
the midst of a society that says the same things. Christians, therefore,
are in the midst of spiritual warfare whether they recognize it or not.

When Jesus was tempted, He used the Word of God in faith and
in relationship to the Father who loved Him. He provided both the
example and the way. Satan would like Christians with problems to
avoid looking at Jesus and using the Word of God. By enticing
believers to focus on problems or on any number of counterfeit
means of help, Satan distracts them from God's provision of help:

---

2. Ray Stedman, *Folk Psalms of Faith* (Glendale, Calif.: Gospel Light, Regal, 1973), p.
41.
3. Jay E. Adams, *More Than Redemption* (Grand Rapids: Baker, 1979), p. xiii.

Jesus. The writer to the Hebrews encouraged Christians to fix their eyes on Jesus,

> the author and perfecter of faith, who for the joy set before Him endured the cross, despising the shame, and has sat down at the right hand of the throne of God. (Hebrews 12:2)

Once Satan distracts believers from Jesus through deception, he offers all kinds of avenues to so-called mental-emotional healing, all of which end up in self, secular humanism, and idolatry. He continues to argue that God did not really mean what He has said, that we can place our confidence in the ways of the world, and that God does not really love us in mercy and truth.

Believers continually need to turn back to the Word and focus on Jesus, the perfect expression of God's love. Because of His love, God has provided the means to resist temptation and to overcome sin. Besides the procedure demonstrated by Jesus Himself, we have additional instructions in the Word.

> Submit therefore to God. Resist the devil and he will flee from you. Draw near to God and He will draw near to you. (James 4:7-8)

Submitting to God involves believing His love and His Word. It involves believing Him to the point of obeying and thanking Him. When one is truly submitted to God he has the ability and the authority to resist the devil. Therefore, biblical counselors will seek to help their counselees live in submission to God's love, His Word, and His enabling.

Faith to believe and do what is clear in Scripture will cause a person to develop wisdom by which to meet every challenge. The Bible contains both general principles and specific examples having to do with thought and behavior. The Bible is comprehensive, but it is not exhaustive. It is comprehensive in that it tells us generally everything we need to know about thinking and behaving, but it does not tell us specifically what to do in all situations. Because it is comprehensive, we must have as full an understanding of it as possible. Because it is not exhaustive, we must have a relationship with God that fosters individual application. The gap between the general principles of Scripture and the particulars of application is filled by the direction of the Holy Spirit.

In addition to being comprehensive, the Bible speaks to the deepest and most profound levels of life. The spiritual aspects of mankind are not merely positive additives, but rather are the most essential attributes influencing thinking and behaving. The love relationship of God to man is evident throughout Scripture, and it is within this relationship that the problems of living may be met.

Examining the Counselee's Needs

The counselor and counselee need to investigate aspects of creation, separation, and restoration through conversation. The following questions are merely general examples. A counselor should look at these areas in terms of the particular person, situation, and details of need and application.

CREATION

1. *Spiritual nature* of the person. Is he more aware of circumstantial and psychological aspects of the problem than the spiritual implications or possibilities? Is he tending to act more in the flesh than in the spirit? Does the person sense poverty of spirit?

2. *Uniqueness of the person.* Is the counselor attempting to treat this person in the same way as another person with a similar problem? Is the counselee attempting to be like someone else, or is he depressed that he is different from another person? Does he accept the way God made him? Is he appreciative of the way God made him?

3. *Free will and responsibility.* Does the counselee take responsibility for his thoughts, words, and actions, or does he make excuses, justify himself, or blame someone else? Does he feel trapped by circumstances? Is he aware that he continually makes choices? What new choices might he make?

SEPARATION

1. *Faith* (belief versus unbelief). What does the person truly believe about God in relation to this circumstance? Does he believe that God is faithful to help him through the problem (1 Corinthians 10:13)? Does he believe that God will work

something good through the circumstances (Romans 8:28-29)? Does he truly believe that God loves him? What does he believe that might be encouraged?

2. *Hope* (true hope versus false hope and despair). Where does the person's hope for the future lie—in self, circumstances, other people, or God? Is the person hoping to escape consequences, or is he trusting God to work in his life? How does he view life and death? If the person has reached despair, what glimmer of hope might he see in God?

3. *Love* (God's love versus self-love). Does the person understand the basis for God's love? Does he understand the demonstration of God's love through the cross? Does he respond to God's love? Does he love God and others? Is he preoccupied with self? Does he have trouble giving and receiving? Is there a conflict between humility and pride, between obedience and self-will, or between submission and rebellion?

RESTORATION

1. *Death and resurrection of Christ* (new life). Has the person truly received new life by faith in Jesus? Are there areas of sin which need to be confessed and forgiven? Are there aspects of the self which need to be brought to the cross and reckoned dead? Might there be personal hurts that need to be healed? Are there others that this person needs to forgive? Is he walking according to the new creation in Christ or according to the ways of his old nature? Does he put off the old and put on the new in some areas of his life? Does the person live in relationship to God through loving Him in gratitude, in obedience, and in prayer?

2. *Holy Spirit.* Does the person yield himself to the influence of the Holy Spirit in his life? Does he recognize his source for living the Christian life? Or is he ignoring or grieving the Holy Spirit? Does he trust that the Holy Spirit will guide and enable him to do God's will? Does he look to the Holy Spirit to help him understand God's Word and to help him pray?

3. *Word of God.* Does the person feed his new life with the Word of God on a regular basis? What does he believe

concerning what God has said? Does he agree with God's Word, or are there areas of reservation? Does he know what God has said in reference to his own situation? Does he respond to the Word in necessary areas of change? Does he apply the Word in daily situations? How much does he do (obey) in contrast to how much he knows intellectually?

These are just a few questions. Through looking at these areas of creation, separation, and restoration, the counselor may determine whether the counselee is living as though he is separated from God or whether he is living in relationship to God. Either way, the counselor is there to teach and encourage the person to draw closer to God through His means of restoration. Relationship with God enables the person to live as God designed him to live and therefore to meet the challenges of life His way.

OPPORTUNITIES FOR SPIRITUAL GROWTH

Problems of living provide opportunities for spiritual growth. If one has enough money, a peaceful marriage, a satisfying job, and no problems, it is unlikely that he will grow spiritually. Each believer needs to know and understand that problems provide the motivation to draw closer to God and to choose to walk after the Spirit (James 1:2-5).

In our affluent happiness-hunting society, pain and sorrow are considered anathema. Christians need to know that each problem of living has the potential of spiritual growth or decline. As problems affect the flesh there are choices to seek God or to follow the ways of the flesh. Psychological relief through psychological means may merely provide an escape from spiritual growth.

Each problem should motivate an individual into seeking God— not only so that the problem he faces will be solved, but also so that God's will can work in him to transform him through tribulation. Paul found purpose in his troubles:

> Therefore having been justified by faith, we have peace with God through our Lord Jesus Christ . . . and we exult in hope of the glory of God. And not only this, but we also exult in our tribulations, knowing that tribulation brings about perseverance; and perseverance, proven character; and proven character, hope; and hope does not disappoint, because the love of God has been poured out within our hearts through the Holy Spirit who was given to us. (Romans 5:1-5)

Problems of living can indeed strengthen faith, hope, and love as a Christian draws closer to God through his difficulties.

Because biblical methodology of counseling draws a person closer to God, heartaches, suffering, and distress are looked at from God's perspective of love, rather than from a limited human perspective. Jesus suffered because of love. He not only died for the sins of humanity, He experienced the depths of pain through identification with our sin. All of the suffering of mankind was compressed into the few hours of darkness and separation from the Father while Jesus hung on that dreadful instrument of death. Because of the ugliness of sin, love suffers.

Biblical counseling must deal with suffering from a biblical perspective and within the context of God's love. Many Christians desire to know the power of Jesus' resurrection, but few desire to know the "fellowship of His sufferings" (Philippians 3:10). Yet though suffering is not to be sought, it must often be borne. There are many encouragements in Scripture to be longsuffering, to put up with one another, and to bear the pain of living for Christ in a world that either hates or ignores Him. Counseling, therefore, necessarily involves suffering, and the biblical counselor will encourage the person who is suffering to draw closer to God through His love.

Because of His love, God has given us a living hope for a future with Him, a resurrected life throughout which we will be like Jesus and always be with Him. Biblical counseling therefore offers a hope beyond present difficulties. That hope gives the one who suffers courage to face the present, and it fills him with the love of God even in his trials. Counseling the love of God focuses on the future with hope, rather than on the past with determinism or despair.

FULL PROVISION OF LOVE

Counseling the love of God cannot be a narrow methodology because we have not yet fathomed the depths nor reached the heights of His love. Nevertheless, God has given His people the choice and the ability to believe Him, to hope in Him, to love Him, and to follow Him. He has given His church all that believers need to counsel one another through the Word of God and the work of the Holy Spirit.

God provided all that is necessary to draw a person close to Himself. As individuals choose to believe God they draw closer to

Him and in turn grow in their faith. As they hope in the cross of Christ and in the resurrection they draw still closer to God and grow in hope. As they receive God's love in the midst of their problems their spirit is refreshed and they continue to draw closer to God and increase in their love for Him. Each step a person takes in the direction of drawing closer to God through His love increases the person's ability to overcome life's problems with God's wisdom and enabling. Touch the spiritual part of a person's life, and you will be touching the most powerful possibility for change.

The methodology of biblical counseling is actually identical to the methodology of encouraging one another to live the Christian life as it is presented in the Bible. It is therefore a personal application of teaching, preaching, and loving one another as Christ loves us. Indeed, it is as "foolish" as preaching, for it depends upon the power of God and the leading of the Holy Spirit, rather than the clever techniques of men. The work of the counselor in relationship to the love of God is well stated by Larry Christenson:

> The objective of Christian counseling is to help facilitate an encounter between the person being counseled and the Lord, in which the Lord's gracious will in regard to the person may be done.[4]

Because the methodology of biblical counseling is based on relationship with God rather than upon formulas or techniques, there are persons who are already prepared to be counselors. The Holy Spirit has worked in such prospective counselors and has transformed them through His presence and through His Word. Such persons, if they are called and gifted for counseling, will be able to lead a counselee along the path by which the Lord has been leading them. Rather than giving a set of formulas or even a map, the Lord gives us people who have found the way of drawing close to Him through His love (2 Corinthians 1:4, 6). The best guide is the one who has walked in the ways of God, not the one who has simply read charts and studied maps.

This is why we stress that a counseling ministry can begin even before this book has been read, because the means of biblical counseling are already there. We have found in selecting counselors that those who have had life experiences with God, who have grown

4. Larry Christenson, letter to Martin Bobgan and Deidre Bobgan, 7 July 1979.

in those experiences through the enabling of the Holy Spirit, and who have been given the gift of counseling are filled with biblical methodology of change. Even if a counselor does not know specific answers to certain specific problems and even if the Scripture does not deal with the specific problem, he can depend upon the fact that ministry of the Word to the person can help.

THE GOAL

The basic problem with human beings (model of man) is their fallen nature or flesh (separation from God), and the pathway from heartache to health (methodology of change) is paved with God's love. Anything from anxiety to xenophobia can be transformed by God's love. Drawing close to God through His love and responding in faith, hope, and love will help a Christian solve his problems and will conform him to the image of Christ.

Like psychological counseling, spiritual counseling involves listening and learning, gaining understanding into thought and behavior, and discovering and implementing changes. But biblical counseling does even more. It attempts to help the individual into a scriptural awareness and understanding of himself and of God's intentions for him. It leads a person into a deeper knowledge of God and spiritual growth through the death and resurrection of Christ.

Without resorting to psychological models and methods, the church needs to express God's love to those who are suffering from problems of living. In ministering God's love a biblical counselor will rely on the Bible as the primary reference. No other book contains the riches, depths, power, and accuracy of the Word of God. The Bible reveals a reality that is truer than experience; it is the light in a dark world. We cannot find our way out of darkness with more darkness. We need the light of God's Word and the life of His Son, the Living Word.

PART 2

Counselee, Counselor, Conversation

7

The Counselee and Change

For those who are inexperienced in counseling, there is a seeming mystery about it. Two people meet. One has a problem and the other supposedly has the solution. They talk—and talk—and talk—week after week—and month after month—and then hopefully the counselee improves and the two part company. What happens in counseling and how and why people change involve three elements: the counselee, the counselor, and the conversation. Of these three, the counselee is the most important factor.

Biblical counseling centers on a relationship of love which involves both mercy and truth. The primary relationship to consider is that between God and the counselee. God's sovereign will and His grace far outweigh the conversation and the human counselor in importance. Therefore, within the counseling setting, God must have preeminence as the One who created the counselee, the One who provided the way from separation to restoration, and the only One who can transform that person into the image of Jesus. God is the primary counselor, and His presence must be acknowledged throughout the conversation.

> Trust in the Lord with all your heart,
> And do not lean on your own understanding.
> In all your ways acknowledge Him,
> And He will make your paths straight.
> (Proverbs 3:5-6)

Both counselor and counselee need to focus on God in counseling, not just on one another, the problem, or the conversation.

Next to the Lord, the most important, yet most overlooked, person is the counselee. He is the one whom the Lord graciously desires to mold into the image of Christ. In the past, many people have approached counseling as though the counselor and the process of counseling were the major contributions to change. In psychological counseling the therapist has been looked to as a change agent bringing about transformation through his methods and techniques. But it is the counselee's own desire, motivation, and willingness to change that are the key factors.

Even in the psychological realm researchers are now understanding that the counselee's motivation to change and his assuming the responsibility for behavior are far more important than the counselor or the conversation of counseling. The *Handbook of Psychotherapy and Behavior Change* says that what the counselee brings into therapy has the greatest effect on the results.[1] Concerning secular counseling, Thomas Szasz contends:

> If there is any change in the "patient," it is, in the last analysis, brought about by the "patient" himself. Hence, it is false to say that the psychotherapist *treats* or is a therapist. It would be more accurate to say that the "patient" . . . treats himself [emphasis his].[2]

Thus, the counselee and what he brings into a counseling situation are of overwhelming importance.

Biblical counseling goes a step further, however, because of the personal involvement of the Creator. The counselee is still the most important human factor in change, but it is his response to God that contributes to his change. In psychological counseling change occurs when an individual desires to change and takes responsibility to change. In biblical counseling the counselee's desire, motivation, and willingness to take responsibility are also very important, but his relationship to God even surpasses what he himself brings into counseling. Whereas in psychological counseling change occurs through human effort, in biblical counseling the major transforma-

1. Allen E. Bergin and Michael J. Lambert, "The Evaluation of Therapeutic Outcomes," in *Handbook of Psychotherapy and Behavior Change*, ed. Sol L. Garfield and Allen E. Bergin (New York: John Wiley & Sons, 1978), p. 180.
2. Thomas Szasz, *The Myth of Psychotherapy* (Garden City, N.Y.: Doubleday, Anchor, 1978), p. 190.

tion is accomplished by God as a person receives His mercy and truth and chooses to trust and obey.

THE COUNSELEE'S IDENTITY IN CREATION, SEPARATION, AND RESTORATION

Biblical counseling must be spiritual in that it coordinates with God's work in the counselee. Each counselee has been created with a spiritual nature, uniqueness, and free will in order to relate to God in love, to reflect His character, and to respond in obedience. Although all of these attributes have been diminished through sin, God has provided a way through Christ's death and resurrection so that a person may choose to live according to God's plan. God has given the counselee new life to relate in love, He has given the Holy Spirit to enable the counselee to reflect God in individual uniqueness, and He has given the Word to reveal His will and His way.

Various aspects of creation, separation, and restoration are important in looking at the counselee in terms of identity. Who a person is, or who he thinks he is, will influence his choices in thinking, feeling, and acting. If a person looks at himself in terms of the psychological, social self trying to meet his own needs, he misses the reality of his spiritual nature and the miracle of new life in Jesus. If a person attempts to meet life's situations on his own, he will ultimately fail even though he is held responsible for his actions. On the other hand, if he is joined with God through God's provision of restoration, he has new life, the Holy Spirit, and the Bible to enable and guide him in being responsible for his thoughts, emotions, and actions.

IDENTITY: SPIRITUAL NATURE

God created the counselee with a spiritual nature for relationship with Himself. Through the spiritual nature and within this relationship of love, each person was to find his personal identity. Because of separation, however, each person's sense of identity falls short of God's original design. Rather than discovering who he is by responding to God's love in relationship and thereby reflecting Him, each looks to himself, other people, and the world.

Through the centuries each person has based his identity or self-concept upon how he viewed himself and how other people responded to him, rather than on who God is and how God sees him. A person will look at his own characteristics, compare them with others around him, and judge which traits he likes, which ones he rejects, and which ones he wishes he had. These may include personality traits, physical characteristics, mental abilities, and talents. He will determine who he is through interplay with other people and the roles he portrays or through the activities he pursues.

As a person grows from birth through babyhood and then to adolescence and adulthood, he may develop a confident sense of personal identity, a diffident sense of personal identity, or any variation in between. The person with a diffident sense of identity is often unsure and insecure, and he sometimes suffers in various ways through hurt feelings. The person with a confident sense of identity usually feels secure, worthwhile, and generally positive about life.

People with a confident sense of identity are valued and rewarded in society. They are usually the leaders, and they often find themselves in some form of sales or people-oriented enterprise. Those with a diffident sense of identity are usually not in leadership roles, and they are often more pitied than praised. From a human perspective, the individual with a confident identity is much to be preferred over one with a diffident identity. But from a spiritual perspective, neither identity in the flesh is of greater value to God. Neither the confident individual nor the diffident person has the advantage, because both are manifestations of an autonomous personality that finds its confidence or lack of confidence in self.

The great advantage occurs in either case when the individual permits God to take those characteristics and transform them through His love. In each case the characteristics can be transformed by God's love to result in a confident *spiritual* identity.

When an individual receives Jesus by faith, he actually becomes a new creation. "Therefore if any man is in Christ, he is a new creature; the old things passed away; behold, new things have come" (2 Corinthians 5:17). No longer is he an independent, autonomous sinner attempting to establish his own identity and meet his own needs. He is linked with his Creator in vital dependence, for God has taken up residence in the very depths of his being so that he is now no longer his own. He belongs to God, and the source of his new life is God Himself. Paul expressed the idea this way:

I am crucified with Christ; nevertheless I live; yet not I, but Christ liveth in me; and the life which I now live in the flesh I live by the faith of the

Son of God, who loved me, and gave himself for me. (Galatians 2:20, KJV)

Not I, but Christ! In the wonder of His love, Jesus came to dwell within the believer. The mystery of the believer's life is truly "Christ in you, the hope of glory." The believer's identity is not the independent self but the new self, dependent on the life of the indwelling Christ and choosing God's will over self-will.

> If any one wishes to come after Me, let him deny himself, and take up his cross, and follow Me. For whoever wishes to save his life shall lose it; but whoever loses his life for My sake shall find it. (Matthew 16:24-25)

As a believer yields himself to the indwelling Holy Spirit, he becomes more and more like Jesus. His identification with Jesus becomes the essence of his own identity.

As the believer puts on the new life he becomes dependent upon Jesus. That dependence is not passive, however; it does not consist of sitting back and letting God do everything. Rather, it is the active dependence exemplified in the life of Jesus when He said, "My Father is working until now, and I Myself am working" (John 5:17). Jesus' life as a man was both active and effective because the source of all He did and said came from the heart and will of the Father.

Because a Christian is dependent on the Lord in every aspect of life, he needs to consciously and continually purpose to live in Jesus—in the abiding that Jesus talked about:

> Abide in Me, and I in you. As the branch cannot bear fruit of itself, unless it abides in the vine, so neither can you, unless you abide in Me. I am the vine, you are the branches; he who abides in Me, and I in him, he bears much fruit; for apart from Me you can do nothing. (John 15:4-5)

A biblical counselor will encourage a counselee to abide in Jesus, to contemplate the character of Jesus, and to reflect Him. This does not mean thinking merely, *Jesus is kind; therefore I should be kind,* but rather *Jesus is living in me, and He is kind. Therefore, if I am to express Christ in me, I will be kind, not by my own human effort, but by faith in His life in me.* Thus, the transformation takes place through allowing Jesus' life to manifest itself through a human vessel. The power to live the

Christian life does not reside in self but in Him; not by self-will but by His will.

Each character quality of Jesus is consistent with His life within believers. Jesus is perfect love; He is holy, seated at the right hand of the Father, making intercession for us. Ephesians 2:6 says that believers are with Him in the heavenlies; therefore, they can also intercede for others. Just as Jesus forgives, they also can forgive because that is the nature of Jesus in them. Just as they see Jesus' humility, they can reflect His humility as they depend on His life. As they see Him obedient to the Father, they also can be obedient to the Father because of His life within them.

Until a counselee has a strong grasp of who Jesus is in him and who he is in Christ, there should be continual teaching in this most essential area. Descriptions of the new identity can be seen throughout the New Testament. Paul describes the establishment of the new identity in Romans 6 through 8. The epistle to the Ephesians also includes much on the identity of the believer: chosen, accepted in the beloved, redeemed, renewed in the spirit of the mind, putting off old ways and putting on the new. In order to practice walking according to the life of Jesus living within the believer, one must know that He is there to love, guide, enable, and supply all that is necessary to live according to God's will. As a believer discovers the truth of Christ in him and of his position in Christ, he lives according to a new identity that transcends his former self.

IDENTITY: UNIQUENESS

God created each person as a unique vessel for His Spirit. He made each person with certain qualities, distinct physical features, and abilities. Rejection of what God created each person to be or rejection of those qualities that are yet imperfect brings emptiness, envy, unthankfulness, self-pity, and much unhappiness. Those qualities and characteristics are to be relinquished to Him to fill and to use. Whenever people try to change themselves, they are prone to change the very characteristics God has given them. Each counselee must be encouraged to be in cooperation with Jesus and to allow God to transform him according to *His* plan. Rather than trying to replace basic qualities and abilities, a biblical counselor will assist an individual in letting Jesus fill those traits and talents and transform them from within.

IDENTITY: FREE WILL AND RESPONSIBILITY

Throughout the New Testament, believers are encouraged to put off the old self and put on the new. Although through the new birth we are given new life with a new identity, we still have a choice whether to live according to the old ways or according to the new. Paul urged Christians not to walk as unbelievers "in the futility of their mind, being darkened in their understanding, excluded from the life of God, because of the ignorance that is in them, because of the hardness of their heart," but enjoined them instead, "in reference to [their] former manner of life, [to] lay aside the old self, which is being corrupted in accordance with the lusts of deceit, and be renewed in the spirit of your mind, and *put on the new self*, which in the likeness of God has been created in righteousness and holiness of the truth" (Ephesians 4:17-18, 22-24, emphasis added). This appropriation is a continual choice for the believer, and it will affect his ongoing growth in becoming more like Jesus.

Such putting off and putting on has to do with identity in relationship, but it also has to do with external activity. Paul exhorted:

> Do not lie to one another, since you laid aside the old self with its evil practices, and have put on the new self who is being renewed to a true knowledge according to the image of the One who created him. (Colossians 3:9-10)

Inner change comes through the indwelling Holy Spirit, and outer change conforms to His inner life.

Unless a believer knows who he is in Christ, he will attempt to live the Christian life with the same resources he used before knowing Jesus. It is possible for a person to lose sight of Jesus' constant availability to enable him to do God's will. Any form of counseling that does not emphasize the believer in Christ and Christ in the believer will fall short of the essence of Christianity.

As a counselee believes and receives the love of God, he is enabled by the Holy Spirit to trust and obey God. But the will of the counselee is a powerful force, and it can lead him to embrace or resist change. God's love enables a person to choose to trust and obey, but God does not force obedience. He has given the counselee the choice.

Therefore, every counselee takes the responsibility to participate with the Lord in the process. This is not an independent form of responsibility, but rather responsibility to act in dependence upon the Lord, in trust and obedience. The counselee who will benefit most from biblical counseling is the one who is willing to see his problem in the light of Scripture and to seek biblical solutions, who chooses to change through God's love, and who is willing to be responsible for his thinking and acting within the context of God's mercy and truth.

The general responsibility of the counselee to recognize his part in the counseling process has at least the three aspects summarized below.

1. *Positive change occurs when the counselee is willing to see his problem in the light of Scripture and to seek biblical solutions.* A counselee who will benefit from biblical counseling needs to be willing to see the spiritual basis of problems of living. He must be willing to look below the surface of the problem to what aspect of his character the Lord would like to change. In addition, he must be willing to seek spiritual solutions involving the mercy and truth of God, but also involving putting off the old ways of thinking, feeling, and behaving and putting on the ways of God as revealed in the Bible.

The Bible deals with all essential aspects of living, is a guide for righteous living, and presents the reasons underlying wrong living. Problems that surface in thinking and behaving actually involve the spiritual realm. When an individual does not trust God, he has a spiritual problem that will affect much of his thinking and behaving. When there is fear, anxiety, pride, lust, self-centeredness, unforgiveness, rebellion, resentment, or bitterness at the root of external problems, a counselee needs to be willing to see his problems as spiritual ones for which there are spiritual solutions. He can then come into a deeper relationship with the Lord as he involves God in the solutions. But if he sees his problems as psychological, self-effort may be attempted in the solution, and spiritual transformation can be delayed or prevented.

2. *Positive change occurs when the counselee chooses to change through God's love.* In most cases a counselee knows what to do but does not do it. As the counselee moves from his own ways (self-love) to God's ways (through His mercy and truth), he will be able both to know and to do. The stronger the desire to change, the less help is needed. Increase a person's desire to change and you decrease his need for counseling. All the training in Bible verses and all the encouraging in

biblical directions will do nothing until the counselee desires to change.

People vary in their reaction to change. Some persons claim that they want to change, but they actually do not. They want some external force to change them or to change their circumstances. Others are openly unwilling to change, and some are even unwilling to recognize resistance to change within themselves. Because of the risk involved, they want to avoid change at any cost. Psychological counselors have noted the paradox of individuals who come into counseling to change and then proceed to do all they can to resist changing. One wonders why these people engage in counseling if they do not intend to change. One psychiatrist offered this explanation: They come for counseling in order to "go through the motions of changing while confirming that they have no real intention of ever really doing so."[3] Then there are those who feel they have been forced into counseling. They are not there because they want to be. Such people may do all they can to prove that counseling is not what they need.

Whatever the basis of resistance to change, help cannot be imposed upon those who do not wish to receive it. No one can compel another to change. John Gedo says of psychological counseling that "to require patients to improve is an illegitimate infringement on their autonomy."[4] The same is true of biblical counseling. Compulsory counseling, like compulsory confession in the church, is self-defeating. It is best to wait for willing cooperation and motivation.

Love is the primary motivating force for change. As a person learns about, believes, and experiences the love, patience, kindness, and gentleness of God, he will have the security necessary to choose new thoughts and actions.

Some Christians can apply God's love to other Christians but cannot apply His love to themselves. Often they are looking in the wrong direction—at themselves rather than at God. When a person looks at himself he may not see how God can love him, but that is the wonder of the greatness of God's love. Another reason they may not be open to believing God's love is that they have not received

3. Eric Marcus, "The Use of Paradox," *Association for Humanistic Psychology Newsletter,* December 1982, p. 6.
4. John Gedo, "A Psychoanalyst Reports at Mid-Career," *The American Journal of Psychiatry* 136, no. 5: 649.

much love from people. That is why Jesus stressed the importance of Christians loving one another just as He loved them. Some people are afraid to believe God's love for fear that it might not last. They need to hear more about God and experience consistent caring in the church.

A counselee who believes God's love and responds to that love in trust and obedience will quickly receive instruction in counseling and will greatly benefit from the counsel of the Word of God. A person who is well-founded in the love of God and in a personal relationship with Him may only need direction as to how best to handle a situation. He will be willing to bear the pain for the sake of another; he will be willing to forgive, to forbear, to exercise patience, and to love in the most difficult circumstances. Nevertheless, even those who are well-related to God in love may need the counsel and support of a biblical counselor while going through difficult trials. Such people, as they receive and respond to the love of God through trials, become vessels of blessing to others and glorify God.

3. *Positive change occurs when a counselee is willing to be responsible for his thinking, feeling, and acting within the context of God's mercy and truth.* Many people do resist taking responsibility for their thinking, feeling, and acting. Either they say they cannot help what they think, feel, and do, or they blame circumstances or other people. For some, this resistance occurs because it would be too devastating for them to do otherwise. They cannot take personal responsibility without at the same time experiencing a horrible sense of self-condemnation, discouragement, and defeat. Therefore the counselee needs to be encouraged and motivated, within the context of mercy and truth, to accept responsibility for desires, attitudes, thoughts, words, or deeds. Otherwise positive change will not occur.

The biblical counselor's relationship to the counselee in the matter of accepting personal responsibility for one's choices is different from the relationship the professional counselor has to the counselee. In professional counseling there is often a responsibility placed upon and received by the therapist. He is asked to wave his "magic wand" of theories and perform with his grab bag of techniques in order to "heal" the patient. After all, isn't that what he's paid for? Because psychotherapists charge a fee, they are forced to accept the responsibility for change.

Biblical counselors do not have this problem. They do have a responsibility, but it is not to change the counselee. Rather, their responsibility is to encourage, to listen, to teach, to exhort, to enlighten, to persuade, and to reveal God, all in the love of God expressed in mercy and truth. The counselor helps bear another's burdens so that the counselee will be able to bear his own burdens in the Lord (Galatians 6:5)—for how can the conversation of counseling be of much help unless the counselee decides to cooperate with God?

Not only does the counselee have to take responsibility for what he is already doing, but he has to take responsibility for changing certain forms of thinking, feeling, and acting. Those who will actually do something different will accomplish change. That action may take many forms. For one person, it may take the form of choosing to hold a certain truth about God in the mind; or for another, it may take the form of choosing to be kind to a particular person. Whatever the choice, each time a counselee takes responsibility to cooperate with the Lord through specific obedience, he changes and grows. Often we give a counselee specific activities to do. Those who do them experience improvement, but those who say they tried to do them but could not find the time or get up the motivation to carry through often stay right where they are. Also, those who do them only through self-effort, without involving God, may have only superficial change.

APPLYING THE PRINCIPLES OF CHOICE, RESPONSIBILITY, AND CHANGE

Quite often the major reason people engage in counseling is to have the other person change. This is especially true of marriage counseling. Each partner hopes that the other one is hearing what he or she needs to do rather than taking personal responsibility. Yet if the attention can be taken away from what the other person should do, or away from negative circumstances, the individual can begin to look to the Lord to bring about necessary personal changes. Consequently, we apply the principles of choice, responsibility, and change by asking the following question of the counselee: Are you willing to change even if the other person (such as spouse, boss, or friend) or circumstances do not change? This question forces the counselee to move outside the shelter of blame for others he has erected. It makes him face responsibility for his life even if he has been terribly wronged by those about him.

In blaming another, a person places responsibility for his

problems on someone other than himself and thus tries to exonerate himself from accountability. But rather than gaining from such a shift of responsibility, the person who blames others actually prevents himself from learning and growing. He lets himself get caught, for example, in the trap of blaming his parents for his condition, rather than taking the kind of responsibility for present choices of thinking and acting that an adult characteristically takes. He remains childish when he could choose to forgive his parents in the grace and power of Christ.

Blame began in the Garden and has continued throughout the generations. When Cain's sacrifice was unacceptable to God, he blamed Abel in his heart rather than taking responsibility for his own choice of sacrifice. The Israelites blamed Moses and God for the discomforts of the forty years in the wilderness rather than taking responsibility for obeying God and entering the Promised Land.

Joseph could have spent all of his time and emotional energy blaming his brothers for his troubles and ended up a bitter, hostile old man. But instead he trusted God, took responsibility for his own actions, and forgave his brothers. David could have blamed Bathsheba for enticing him, but instead he took the responsibility for his sin, confessed, and received the forgiveness and mercy of God.

A person cannot easily move ahead in responsible choices if he is blaming others for his problems. Nor can a person receive forgiveness and cleansing if he is blaming someone else instead of confessing, repenting, and choosing to change with God's grace. Much encouragement may be needed to move a person away from blaming into taking responsibility. One way to bring attention away from blame to responsibility is to ask, "What can *you* do to change the situation (or relationship)?" And then together the counselor and counselee may look at areas of change in the context of God's love and His Word. The individual needs to examine how God can work in his life so that he can change his thoughts, attitudes, and actions or so that he can change his responses and reactions. In every case of counseling we focus on what God would expect a person to do and especially that God can help him do it.

One serious pattern of blame is that of the hurt-victim, one who feels hurt and helpless. He seeks persons to help him feel better and to rescue him out of circumstances in which he feels helpless. Although he seeks loving care, the hurt-victim cannot easily receive love because he always fears that the one who expresses love will also hurt him. Thus the hurt-victim has a confused version of God—one moment Savior and the next moment hurter. Family, friends, counselor, and God may be seen alternately as helping friends or hurting enemies.

The hurt-victim views God and others as helpers when they are pleasing him and making him feel good, but as hurters when they are not pleasing him or making him feel good. The manipulative pattern involves three implications:

> I hurt; please help me.
> I hurt; don't hurt me.
> I hurt; you hurt me.

Hurt becomes closely aligned with the hurt-victim's will being done. Furthermore, the hurt must be sustained to develop and maintain relationships. Although the hurt-victim wants to feel better, he fears losing the help and may intensify the hurt feelings to increase involvement of relationship. If the counselee reacts to helpful truth and suggestions for changes in thinking and behaving with more hurt, then he is solidifying the hurt-victim stance and will respond to the counselor as though he is the hurter rather than a helper.

Often a person enmeshed in the hurt feelings of self-pity does not see God's love and fears that God will hurt rather than help. He does not recognize God's love because he sees himself as a victim rather than a sinner. After all, if one is a victim he cannot be responsible for thoughts, emotions, words, or actions. The hurt-victim may honestly believe that he cannot help what he does and may think that he is "good" because he is doing the best he can in spite of his hurt and fear. It's the ultimate blame game with the weapons of hurt and fear. And the saddest aspect of the victim role is that if he does not recognize himself as a sinner, he can never fully know the love of God, who gave Himself as a Lamb to be slain. Jesus came to save sinners, not victims.

Until a person faces and admits his sin and separation from God he cannot receive the forgiveness and restoration God makes available through Jesus. Thus, if a person blames other people or circumstances, or if a person sees himself more as a victim than a sinner, he remains in his sins and cannot truly know the love of God. Although blaming another person and playing the role of victim postpones facing one's own responsibilities, such a person wraps coils of self-deception around himself that will cause him great harm.

Jesus has given Christians the opportunity and ability to be victors instead of victims, even in the worst of circumstances. One who has habitually played the hurt-victim role may move out of that role through choosing to act differently toward others. By following principles found in such Scriptures as Romans 12:14-21, Ephesians 4:22-24, 31-32, and 1 Peter 2:20-24, Christians can respond to wrongdoing in the same manner as Jesus did.

The Lord is in the process of conforming every believer into the image of Christ. Every person needs a good deal of transformation, and God allows people and circumstances to come into a person's life to effect the change. If a person is always looking for change outside himself, he loses the opportunity to grow and thus make positive use out of problems. In fact, if a person waits for others or surroundings to change, he may wait a lifetime. On the other hand, when a believer looks at Jesus and then at himself in the context of God's love, he is encouraged to become more like Him.

The counselee may also try to shift responsibility for change onto the counselor. The counselor needs to see that such a shift is rebuffed. Scripture is clear on the principle of personal responsibility, even in the counseling situation. In Galatians 6:1-9 we see the role of the counselor as helping another to bear his burdens in times of weakness, difficulty, or stress. But even though the counselor comes alongside to help bear the burden, the ultimate responsibility is with the counselee.

> But let each one examine his own work, and then he will have reason for boasting in regard to himself alone, and not in regard to another. For each one shall bear his own load. . . .
>
> Do not be deceived, God is not mocked; for whatever a man sows, this he will also reap. For the one who sows to his own flesh shall from the flesh reap corruption, but the one who sows to the Spirit shall from the Spirit reap eternal life. (Galatians 6:4-5, 7-8)

There is great temptation for a counselor to take more responsibility for a counselee than he should. Some counselees would rather not take responsibility for their actions. They come to a counselor hoping that the counselor will change them. But the counselor cannot violate the free will given to each person by God. Only the counselee can decide to change, and only the counselee can choose to believe God.

The counselor needs to remember that every problem in a person's life is a point of choice. Every situation is an opportunity to trust and obey God. Each point of choice can bring a person closer to mental-emotional stability or mental-emotional disaster. As a person trusts God, is renewed in the spirit of his mind, and obeys God, he proves his own work, establishes his identity in God, and rejoices in that he is assuming responsibility.

The will of the counselee is a powerful force for change. As a Christian chooses to submit to God and chooses to act according to the power of the Holy Spirit living within him, the Lord will accomplish the change. The counselor needs to assess the willingness of the individual to cooperate with the Lord and to follow the spiritual principles of Scripture. Where there is a misunderstanding or lack of knowledge, the counselor will need to instruct. Where there is weakness of will, the counselor will need to encourage. Where there is lack of trust, the counselor will need to love in mercy and truth. Where there is willingness to trust and obey God, the counselor will need only to point the way. When the counselee aligns his will with the will of God, transformation will occur.

As the counselee sees the spiritual nature of his problem, not only through conversation in counseling, but through drawing nearer to God, he will be ready to cooperate with God as He brings the transformation. As the counselee sees God's possibilities for change, he will desire to change. As he comes to know God better, as his eyes are opened to what God desires to do in his life, and as he believes in the available power of God, he will have the security, the motivation, and the ability to change. An encounter with the living Lord Jesus, not only at salvation, but repeatedly and continuously throughout life, is the means for spiritual change and growth that affects all other aspects of living.

8

The Counselor and Change

God calls and prepares all Christians to be vessels of His love and counsel. Some individuals are particularly called and gifted to counsel those who are experiencing problems of living. He teaches them in His Word and His ways so that they, in turn, may instruct and encourage others to know and follow God. A biblical counselor may be either a pastor or lay person. Because of the counselor's dependence on God, he should say along with Paul:

> And such confidence we have through Christ toward God. Not that we are adequate in ourselves to consider anything as coming from ourselves, but our adequacy is from God, who also made us adequate as servants of a new covenant, not of the letter, but of the Spirit; for the letter kills, but the Spirit gives life. (2 Corinthians 3:4-6)

The counseling process and the characteristics of the counselor are intimately interwoven both in Scripture and in practice. What the counselor does cannot be separated from how he does it and who he is. Even in secular, psychological counseling researchers have discovered that the personal qualities of the counselors are far more important than other factors, such as techniques and training.

In biblical counseling the message is Christ, and the counselor depends on "Christ in you, the hope of glory." Psychiatrist Frank Minirth says, "Living the Word of God is much more basic to helping people than psychology will ever be." He says that a Christian leader or a pastor who honors the Word of God and in whose life the Scriptures are working can probably "help ninety-five percent of the people who come to him." Minirth adds that such counselors "need to know that their 'success rate' may be proportionately higher than other professionals."[1]

The biblical counselor is responsible to maintain his own walk with the Lord so that he will think, speak, act, and love more according to the life of the Lord Jesus within him than according to his own fleshly nature. On the one hand, he is to be a living example of the life of Christ and to follow Paul's admonition to Timothy to "show yourself an example of those who believe" (1 Timothy 4:12). On the other hand, he must not deceive himself into thinking that he is beyond temptation or that he is in any way superior to the counselee. A spirit of meekness and dependence on the Lord is essential because of the temptation to think that a counselor is able to help another person because of his own merit or abilities. Because a biblical counselor represents the Lord in counseling, he must constantly live according to Galatians 2:20:

> I have been crucified with Christ; and it is no longer I who live, but Christ lives in me; and the life which I now live in the flesh I live by faith in the Son of God, who loved me, and delivered Himself up for me.

A spiritual counselor fulfills the law of Christ, which is basically the law of love, by assisting another person to bear his burdens and to grow in the Lord. Such interpersonal qualities extend beyond human warmth and empathy and provide the atmosphere for the work of the Holy Spirit in the counselee. Not only will these qualities help a counselee to grow and change; they will also help the person to know the character of God as seen through a human vessel.

THE COUNSELOR AND FAITH, HOPE, AND LOVE

The counselor's faith in the sufficiency of God is imperative as he attempts to help people move toward wholeness, to look to God for guidance and strength, to grow in faith, and to walk in the Spirit.

1. Frank Minirth, "The Demands, Dilemmas, and Dangers of Pastoral Counseling," *Leadership*, Fall 1980, p. 132.

Without faith in God's Word, in God's transforming power, and in God's purposes for each individual, the counselor will falter and begin to counsel the ways of men. Without hope for growth and change, he will become fainthearted and weary in well doing. And without love he will degenerate into critic instead of counselor. Just as "the just shall live by faith," so the biblical counselor must counsel by faith. Just as the counselor has been given a blessed hope, so he is to minister in hope.

The counselor needs to believe in his heart that God is true and faithful in all circumstances and that nothing is impossible with Him. The spiritual counselor must depend on and teach the truth of Romans 8:28-29.

> And we know that God causes all things to work together for good to those who love God, to those who are called according to His purpose. For whom He foreknew, He also predestined to become conformed to the image of His Son, that He might be the first-born among many brethren.

As the counselor keeps the Lord in prominent view and remembers that God allows circumstances (even adverse ones) for a person's growth in becoming like Jesus, he will be providing hope for the counselee and courage through the trials he faces. The counselor recognizes that problems can be an obstacle or catalyst to Christian growth, depending upon one's response to the problems and to the Lord. Even though he may identify with compassion, the counselor is to look beyond the circumstances to possibilities for growth and change. In this way he will be able to help the individual capitalize on circumstances, benefit from pain and discomfort, exercise faith in the midst of confusion, and enter Christ's victory in the midst of adverse situations. Everything in a Christian's life is used by God to bring the new creature into full maturity. The biblical counselor desires to cooperate with this goal. He needs to ask, *How can God use this problem creatively in this Christian's life so that not only is the problem handled, but the individual grows more like Jesus in the process?*

"But now abide faith, hope, love, these three; but the greatest of these is love" (1 Corinthians 13:13). Love is what biblical counseling is all about. Jesus commanded His followers to love one another just as He had loved them. If a biblical counselor does not love the counselee, he will not be able to be a channel of God's grace to the counselee. Paul's words to the Colossians aptly apply to counselors:

And so, as those who have been chosen of God, holy and beloved, put on a heart of compassion, kindness, humility, gentleness and patience; bearing with one another, and forgiving each other, whoever has a complaint against any one; just as the Lord forgave you, so also should you. And beyond all these things put on love, which is the perfect bond of unity. And let the peace of Christ rule in your hearts, to which indeed you were called in one body; and be thankful. Let the word of Christ richly dwell within you, with all wisdom teaching and admonishing one another with psalms and hymns and spiritual songs, singing with thankfulness in your hearts to God. And whatever you do in word or deed, do all in the name of the Lord Jesus, giving thanks through Him to God the Father. (Colossians 3:12-17)

Love is communicated through the look in the eyes, the interest in the counselee, and the gentle touch. But the greatest communication of love is not something that can be learned by rote or put on. Genuine love has a way of coming through if indeed the counselor loves God with all his heart, soul, mind, and strength and his neighbor as himself. God's love reaches into the heart of a counselee when it is flowing through the person who speaks.

Although the counselor may naturally care for and appreciate qualities of the counselee, the love he gives the counselee should originate more from his own love relationship with God than from anything about the counselee. That will protect the counselor from becoming discouraged when progress is slow and from becoming personally hurt if a counselee expresses critical or angry feelings toward him. When Jesus gave Peter the responsibility to feed His sheep, He based it upon Peter's love for Him. He asked, "Simon, son of John, do you love Me more than these?" When Peter replied, "Yes, Lord; You know that I love you," Jesus said, "Tend My lambs" (John 21:15). The questioning was repeated along with the admonition to shepherd the sheep. To be a shepherd, Peter had to love Jesus more than anyone else and more than life itself. The same is true of biblical counselors.

Jesus said, "This is My commandment, that you love one another, just as I have loved you" (John 15:12). His love is a balance of mercy and truth. When a counselor lives in the context of biblical love he will be sensitive to the counselee's needs. He will communicate love by being available, listening, identifying with the counselee, attempting to understand, and teaching the truth that will benefit the counselee. No matter what kind of person the counselee may be at the moment, the biblical counselor will treat him with respect and esteem, for Paul wrote:

> Do nothing from selfishness or empty conceit, but with humility of mind let each of you regard one another as more important than himself; do not merely look out for your own personal interests, but also for the interests of others. (Philippians 2:3-4)

Biblical love takes time, commitment, involvement, and the giving of self. Jesus said, "I am the good shepherd; the good shepherd lays down His life for the sheep" (John 10:11).

Because biblical counseling is not protected by the professional stance of not becoming personally involved with the counselee or by the external boundaries of payments and appointment schedules, a biblical counselor cannot have a vast number of counselees. Therefore, the ministry of biblical counseling must be shared among the members of the body.

SHORTCOMINGS OF PROFESSIONAL LOVE

Although psychotherapists may care for and love some of their clients, they may actually detest others. The therapist may react to the distorted personality of the client in such a way as to subtly convey dislike and rejection. Furthermore, even for those patients whom he likes, the psychotherapist has limited his practice to a paid relationship fixed by time and fee. Such a limited relationship can hardly communicate the kind of love and care that people who are suffering desperately need. One wonders what kind of involvement, concern, and real love can be given by a profession in which almost half of the psychotherapists in one large study "are sufficiently dissatisfied with their profession that they would not reenter it if they were to live their lives again."[2]

Furthermore, love in secular counseling may be distorted into sexual exploitation. One study of psychotherapists indicated that "more than one out of 10 admitted erotic contact with patients, including acts just short of intercourse," and "more than one out of 20 admitted actual sexual intercourse. Of these therapists, 80 percent acknowledged involvement with more than one patient." It must be

---

2. E. Lowell Kelly et al., "Twenty-five Years Later," *The American Psychologist* 33, no. 8 (August 1978): 752.

that this is a conservative figure, since many therapists would no doubt not admit to such activity. One former psychology professor who has studied the subject said about the above figures, "I think it's probably twice that."[3] With respect to these sexual contacts, it is known that "the vast majority of the unethical therapists were men (96 percent) seducing patients who are women."[4] The *Los Angeles Times* reports that "the American Psychological Association appears unable to police its membership."[5] Besides these examples, numerous books by Szasz, Torrey, Laing, Robitscher, and others have detailed many other abuses by therapists.

The professional therapist's desire for as large an income as possible leads him to maximize his contacts with patients. The more appointments, the greater the income. Many therapists not only work eight-to-five Monday-through-Friday, but additionally see patients on evenings and on Saturdays. This compulsion to increase contacts for the sake of income is one of the major detriments of the psychological way. In practice, it requires that a patient enter the office on the hour and leave fifty minutes later. This pattern is repeated forty times per week and sometimes more through the evening hours and on Saturdays. As we have said elsewhere: "A psychotherapist must fill enough fifty-minute hours to make a desirable income. Thus psychotherapy is a business that tends to revolve around time and money, rather than around people and love."[6] Such a system can only be financially rewarding to the therapist and detrimental to the client.

Once a therapeutic relationship has been established there is a genuine incentive (income) for the therapist to continue it and often a genuine need in the patient to return (because of the dependency relationship he has established with the therapist). When a person has shared deeply with a therapist, a bonding occurs that is hard to break. We have been told by individuals that it was not only difficult to break the relationship but that withdrawal pains occurred when the break was finally made. Research does not support long-term

3. Elaine Warren, "Sex in Therapy: When Ethics Fade," *Los Angeles Herald Examiner*, 26 November 1978, p. A-12.
4. Elaine Woo, "Sex and the Psychotherapist; A New Study on Cause, Effect," *Los Angeles Herald Examiner*, 28 August 1981, p. A-1.
5. Lois Timnick, "Psychologists Face Identity Crisis," *Los Angeles Times*, 14 September 1981, part 1, p. 3.
6. Martin Bobgan and Deidre Bobgan, *The Psychological Way/The Spiritual Way* (Minneapolis: Bethany Fellowship, 1979), p. 157.

psychotherapeutic relationships, however. Two Harvard Community Health Plan psychiatrists report in the *American Journal of Psychiatry* that in their experience "only 1%–2% of patients require long-term continuous psychotherapy."[7] The *Handbook of Psychotherapy and Behavior Change* reports: "Clearly, long-term psychotherapy is difficult to justify on the basis of research reports when they are compared with briefer treatment approaches."[8] Two writers dramatize the truth of this research by stating that "there is little hard evidence that a year of deep analysis is any more salving to the psyche than a week of deep body massage."[9] Yet, disregarding this research, psychotherapists tend to service patients as long as the fees continue to be paid.

In addition to the various abuses, the psychotherapeutic setting provides only a highly contrived and restricted relationship. The likelihood of a professional counselor having more than a fifty-minute, once-per-week interest in anyone is almost nil. A female therapist once told us about a female client's calling on the telephone and asking her to lunch. The therapist gently, but firmly, said, "Thank you, but I cannot do that. I'm your therapist and not your friend." Even if a therapist wanted to be a friend to a patient outside of the office, the forty-plus patient-per-week work load would no doubt prohibit it. Biblical counseling, because it is a shared responsibility of the Body of Christ, should not be offered on such a treadmill of appointments as is done in psychological counseling. Because biblical counseling occurs according to need and because members of the Body come together at occasions other than counseling times, the effect of the personal qualities of the spiritual counselor can exceed the fifty-minute boundaries.

If conversation can cure, the person can be better ministered to by the Body of Christ. The contrast between a fifty-minute, once-per-week talk session with a paid listener (who is obligated by financial necessity and a calendar of appointments to listen to forty to fifty persons per week) and a body of believers available for more than a brief single time slot (who minister freely, unconstrained by

7. Michael Bennett and M. J. Wisneski, "Continuous Psychotherapy Within an HMO," *American Journal of Psychiatry* 136, no. 10 (October 1979): 1283.
8. Allen E. Bergin and Michael J. Lambert, "The Evaluation of Therapeutic Outcomes," in *Handbook of Psychotherapy and Behavior Change*, ed. Sol Garfield and Allen Bergin (New York: John Wiley & Sons, 1978), p. 170.
9. David Gelman and Mary Hager, "Psychotherapy in the '80's," *Newsweek*, 30 November 1981, p. 73.

the necessity to generate an income or to see large numbers for the sake of an income) is great to say the least. The church, through its counseling ministry, expands the possibilities for improvement by increasing the number of counselors available and consequently the resources that can be brought to the problem. A psychotherapist cannot take the time or the money to minister the way the Body of Christ can, and in most cases a talk therapist is less well equipped than is the church to meet the broader needs of the one who comes for help.

A church counseling ministry can provide so much more than psychotherapy for those suffering from problems of living. The interpersonal qualities necessary for effective counseling are those very qualities that come with spiritual growth. Furthermore, God can give counselors a special love for people. Jesus calls us to love one another as He loves us. The spiritual counselor has himself found Christ to be the answer to His own problems and spiritual principles to be effective for personal growth.

PSYCHOLOGICAL TRAINING

One of the prime reasons a pastor or a church member will avoid beginning a counseling ministry is because of the lack of psychological training. This fear is unfounded, according the research in the field of psychological counseling. Truax and Mitchell state:

> There is no evidence that the usual traditional graduate training program has any positive value in producing therapists who are more helpful than nonprofessionals.[10]

After reviewing a vast amount of psychotherapy outcome research, Morris Parloff admits that there is no

> convincing evidence that these procedures can be uniquely applied only by members of professions who have completed specified training programs and have honed their skills by lengthy experience.[11]

10. Truax and Mitchell quoted by Sol Garfield, "Psychotherapy Training and Outcome in Psychotherapy," BMA Audio Cassette #T-305 (New York: Guilford, 1979).
11. Morris B. Parloff, "Psychotherapy and Research: An Anaclitic Depression," *Psychiatry* 43 (November 1980): 288.

According to Jerome Frank, "over six-and-a-half million persons saw mental health specialists in 1978." Then Frank reveals the shocking fact of

> the inability of scientific research to demonstrate conclusively that professional psychotherapists produce results sufficiently better than those of nonprofessionals. [12]

A study of trained and untrained therapists by Hans Strupp at Vanderbilt University compared the mental-emotional improvement of two groups of male college students. Two groups of "therapists" were set up to provide two groups of students with "therapy." The two student groups were equated on the basis of mental-emotional distress as much as possible. The first group of therapists consisted of five psychiatrists and psychologists.

> The five professional therapists participating in the study were selected on the basis of their reputation in the professional and academic community for clinical expertise. Their average length of experience was 23 years.

The second group of "therapists" consisted of seven college professors from a variety of fields, but without therapeutic training. Each untrained "therapist" used his own personal manner of care, and each trained therapist used his own brand of therapy. The students seen by the professors showed as much improvement as those seen by the highly experienced and specially trained therapists. [13]

Psychotherapist Dr. Bernie Zilbergeld, in his book *The Shrinking of America: Myths of Psychological Change,* argues for the idea "that most problems faced by people would be better solved by talking to friends, spouses, relatives or anyone else who appears to be doing well what you believe you're doing poorly." After reviewing a great amount of research, Zilbergeld says:

> If I personally had a relationship problem and I couldn't work it out with my partner, I wouldn't go and see a shrink. I would look around me for the kind of relationship I admire. I wouldn't care if he was a

12. Jerome Frank, "Mental Health in a Fragmented Society: The Shattered Crystal Ball," *American Journal of Orthopsychiatry* 49, no. 3 (July 1979): p. 406.
13. Hans H. Strupp and Suzanne W. Hadley, "Specific vs Nonspecific Factors in Psychotherapy," *Archives of General Psychiatry* 36 (September 1979): p. 1126.

carpenter or a teacher or a journalist . . . or a shrink. That's who I would go to. I want somebody who's showing by [his] life that [he] can do it.[14]

SPIRITUAL TRAINING

A biblical counselor does not need to be trained in psychological counseling, since he is primarily ministering in the spiritual realm, since he teaches and applies the Word of God, and since he depends upon the work of the Holy Spirit. Rather than increasing confidence in biblical counseling, psychological training tends to undermine the training the Lord has already given through years of Bible reading, listening to sermons and Bible teachings, and applying the Scripture in daily life. The confidence of a Biblical counselor cannot reside in theory or techniques, but must reside in the indwelling presence of God Himself and in His effectual, life-giving Word.

The primary training for biblical counselors is in learning how to live in relationship to God in such a way as to reflect His character and to prove His perfect will in day-to-day challenges of living. As the believer studies, understands, and applies the Word of God through obedience to the Lord, he learns how to live according to God's plan. As he learns to live God's way as revealed in Scripture and by the power of the Holy Spirit, he is enabled to guide others along the same path. As long as the counselor personally knows the way through the love of God, through knowledge of the Bible, and through the experience of walking after the Spirit, he will be able to lead others if the Lord has called him to that task.

In nearly every fellowship there are mature believers who have been prepared and trained by the Lord and who are now ready to minister if given the opportunity and encouragement. A minister who knows his flock could easily identify people who know the Word, have responded to the work of the Holy Spirit in their lives, and are gifted to minister in this way. Therefore, if there is a need for counseling in his church, he could immediately set up such a ministry, either on a formal basis with specific counselors and procedures or on an informal basis of bringing together a person in need of counsel with one who could provide mercy and truth.

Training in biblical counseling is not made up of a given number of years of schooling or a certain number of courses. Rather,

14. Bernie Zilbergeld quoted by Don Stanley, "OK So Maybe You Don't Need to See a Therapist," *Sacramento Bee*, 24 May 1983, p. B-4.

the training is in living and in sharing within the Body the love and wisdom that comes from above. Preparation includes a working knowledge of the Bible, obedience to the truth of God as applied in the life, opportunities of experience in ministry, and dependence upon the Holy Spirit. A counseling ministry is usually not a ministry of a new believer, but rather of one who has walked in the way for a number of years. The counselor needs to know the Word not only as doctrine, but as living truth in his own life. He needs to know both the principles and the power of the Word.

By knowing and applying God's Word, by abiding in Christ, and by loving fellow Christians, a spiritual counselor is trained by God in ministering to other believers. He should be given experience in counseling a little at a time on an informal basis within the Body of Christ. All believers have opportunities to minister grace to one another as the Lord leads. All are called to exhort and encourage one another. As a person learns to rely on the Holy Spirit in those instances and to extend to others the love and wisdom of the Lord, he should be given more opportunities to minister.

In chapter 6 we observed that the primary principle of biblical counseling is that as a person moves closer to God through His love—which includes both mercy and truth and is expressed through His Word and through His Holy Spirit—that person will change in the areas of thought, emotion, and action. A corollary to this principle is that as a counselor draws closer to God through His love, the death of the flesh and the renewal of the mind provide a reservoir from which the Lord can draw to minister to another in need. Whatever spiritual change God is working or has worked in the counselor can be ministered to the counselee even if there is no relationship between a counselor's area of growth and a counselee's problem. It does not matter what area of a counselor's life has been or is being transformed. God can use it as a means of ministering to the counselee's need.

> But we have this treasure in earthen vessels, that the surpassing greatness of the power may be of God and not from ourselves . . . always carrying about in the body the dying of Jesus, that the life of Jesus also may be manifested in our body. For we who live are constantly being delivered over to death for Jesus' sake, that the life of Jesus also may be manifested in our mortal flesh. *So death works in us, but life in you.* (2 Corinthians 4:7, 10-12, emphasis added)

As the counselor yields himself to God's transforming work, he becomes a vessel for God to work in others as well. We have found that God often uses current areas of growth in the counselor as a means of helping one in need. The prayer life, Bible study, and spiritual growth current in the counselor are the elements the Lord most fully uses in the counselee's life. The best training for the counselor is to continue to grow close to God through His love so that God may minister His life and love through him.

The biblical counselor maintains the standard by relying firmly upon the Word of God and continues to be spiritually sensitive by walking closely with God in faith, hope, and love. As he walks in the Spirit (in the ways of God) rather than according to the flesh (the ways of men), he will be able to counsel according to God's ways.

9

Pairing Partners for Change

In psychological counseling, the counselor acts as one who holds the mysteries of change, and he generally maintains a superior position in relationship to the counselee. In biblical counseling, however, the counselor shares with the counselee the office of the priesthood of all believers. Paul wrote, "Knowledge makes arrogant, but love edifies" (1 Corinthians 8:1). In biblical counseling the counselor shares the love of God with the counselee. Both the counselor and the counselee are children in the family of God. They are partners in the process of change the Lord desires to bring. The counselor is not in a position superior to the one who is being counseled. He and the counselee receive from God. Both are moving toward the same goal: to reflect the life of Christ and to live in relationship with God.

DISTINCTIVENESS IN COUNSELORS

Certain counselors are effective with certain kinds of personalities and certain kinds of problems. Therefore, we prayerfully consider which counselor in our church would fit best with an individual who has requested counseling. After a period of experience, counselors learn the types of problems and people to which they are able to minister.

There is a false belief that one counselor can effectively treat a great variety of individuals and a great variety of problems, regardless of the likes or dislikes and the assets or liabilities of the therapist. There is no scientific evidence for such a point of view. Strupp pointed out that though there is an assumption that psychotherapists deal differently with different problems and are fairly flexible in their treatment, his own research did not confirm that idea. In fact, he found that therapists were fairly inflexible.[1]

A psychotherapist may treat anxiety, shyness, fears, marital problems, drug abuse, alcoholism, sexual disorders, and depression during forty different fifty-minute sessions in a single week. But it is doubtful that one counselor can be stretched that far. It is more likely that the professional counselor often obligates himself to be all things to all people because he needs to maintain a large income or because he fears what referral might imply. Or worse, he may actually believe he can serve all problems and all people.

Because no fee is charged, a biblical counselor does not feel obligated for purposes of income to minister to all persons or to all types of problems. And, because his is a shared ministry, a particular biblical counselor does not have to carry the entire load. It is not a problem for him to refer someone to another counselor, because he is acutely dependent on the Lord rather than on his own abilities. Thus in the church counselees can be assigned to those counselors who would be the most effective.

CONSIDERATIONS THAT SHOULD GUIDE PAIRING

Several considerations determine the pairing of partners in biblical counseling. Those include age, background, culture, interests, education, occupation, and types of problems experienced. In age pairing, the counselor is usually the same age or older than the counselee. But that cannot be a strict rule. Also, years of Christian growth may be considered. Although educational background does not have to be similar, some well-educated counselees could not receive from someone who did not have a college degree. Other counselees might be intimidated by someone who has several college degrees. Also, if the personalities of the counselor and counselee are too similar, the necessary balance may be lacking. If a church has a

---

1. Hans Strupp, "Time Limited Psychotherapy: New Research Evidence," BMA Audio Cassette (New York: Guilford, n.d.).

number of lay counselors, it will have more flexibility in pairing partners.

Aside from the pastoral counseling in the church, we believe that women should minister to women, men should counsel men, and couples should minister to couples. There is little research in the area of the desirability of like-sex counseling and no firm conclusions can be drawn.[2] One study does indicate, however, that like-sex counseling is superior to male-female counseling.[3] In another study, two researchers found that whether the therapist is a man or woman can affect the outcome of treatment for women patients. They indicate that there are positive advantages when women therapists work with women patients.[4] One reason for like-sex pairing is that there is easier identification of counselor with counselee. Much psychotherapeutic theory and practice have been developed by men, even though two-thirds of the people seeking help are women. Lack of understanding by men has led to theories that emphasize masochistic and other tendencies attributed to women.[5] Many contemporary female writers are charging male psychotherapists with inflicting the stereotypes of society upon women, resulting in detrimental therapeutic outcomes.[6]

A woman can more easily relate to the problems of being a woman than a man can, and vice versa. In addition, a woman counselor can directly provide physical comfort to another woman at critical moments in counseling. Because we use the Bible as the guide to spiritual counseling, we attempt to follow those principles set forth in Scripture.

> Older women are to . . . encourage the young women to love their husbands, to love their children, to be sensible, pure, workers at home, kind, being subject to their own husbands, that the word of God may not be dishonored. (Titus 2:3-5)

2. Morris B. Parloff, Irene Elkin Waskow, and Barry E. Wolfe, "Research on Therapist Variables in Relation to Process and Outcome," in *Handbook of Psychotherapy and Behavior Change*, ed. Sol Garfield and Allen Bergin (New York: John Wiley & Sons, 1978) p. 264.
3. Ibid., p. 262.
4. Enrico E. Jones and Christina L. Zoppel, "Impact of Client and Therapist Gender on Psychotherapy Process and Outcome" *Journal of Consulting and Clinical Psychology* 50, no. 2 (1982) 259-72.
5. "Shrinks Lobotomize ERA," *Mother Jones*, July 1980, p. 10.
6. Julia Sherman, "Psychotherapy with Women," BMA Audio Cassette, #T-330. (New York: Guilford, n.d.). Annette M. Brodsky and Rachel Hare-Mustin, *Women and Psychotherapy* (New York: Guilford, 1980).

> But I do not allow a woman to teach or exercise authority over a man. (1 Timothy 2:12)

Furthermore, the examples in Scripture generally indicate that men advised men.

In addition to like-sex counseling, we encourage couples to minister to couples in marriage counseling. In both Genesis and Ephesians, the husband-wife relationship is described as "one flesh." Rather than just being two individuals, a husband and wife together form a new unity in marriage, with balancing qualities. Thus, in couple-to-couple counseling, the elements of both members of the "one flesh" relationship are present. For instance, quite often one partner tends to be more strict and the other more lenient. If a counselor ministers to a couple by himself, he may be able to properly identify only with the quality he possesses and therefore will encourage that particular quality. A woman can explain a woman's point of view, and a man can explain a man's for greater clarity and understanding when the couple being counseled cannot seem to understand or accept each other.

Because pairing of partners is so vital, the person who coordinates the counseling ministry should know the counselors fairly well and prayerfully consider which counselor would be the best. Although several different counselors may work effectively with a particular counselee, the Lord knows which vessel is the right one. Therefore, there must be dependence upon the Lord even in the selection process. When there is a need for a counselor and we call the one whom we believe would be the best, there is absolutely no pressure placed on him because of need. Instead, we ask the counselor to seek guidance from the Lord as to whether or not he will accept the counseling assignment. If the counselor does not have confirmation from the Lord, we receive a "no" as gratefully as when a person says "yes." If a counselor feels pressured to minister to someone, he may not be the one the Lord has appointed for the counselee. As much as is possible, we desire that the Lord pair the counseling partners.

10

Conversation for Change

The conversation of biblical counseling must proceed from the Word and Spirit of God. To counsel the way of the Lord to each particular counselee, the biblical counselor must: (1) pursue the Word, (2) pray for the leading of the Holy Spirit, and (3) present the Lord's way as revealed by the Word and the Spirit. Jesus promised,

> The words that I have spoken to you are spirit and are life. (John 6:63)

> But the Helper, the Holy Spirit, whom the Father will send in My name, He will teach you all things, and bring to your remembrance all that I said to you. (John 14:26)

As a counselor reads and studies the Word under the guidance of the Holy Spirit, he will be accumulating a treasury of life and truth from which to draw during counseling. As he seeks the leading of the Holy Spirit, the Spirit will bring forth truth from the Word, which the counselor will have been studying and learning from in obedience. He will have both the truth and the wisdom to present to the counselee who is seeking the way of the Lord.

PURSUE THE WORD

The biblical counselor's personal study of the Word is vital. The more of the Word he knows and applies in his own life, the more prepared he will be to assist another in the way of the Lord. Out of the reservoir of living the Word of God through the enabling of the Holy Spirit, the counselor will have both the mercy and truth of God to minister to another in need. Furthermore, he will be able to lead the counselee into the pursuit of the Word for himself.

Biblical counseling begins with the Word of God. This does not mean a quick and easy answer from the Bible, but a sought-for, lived-through application of Scripture. The biblical counselor must continually pursue the Word and encourage the counselee to do likewise. We cannot stress too strongly the importance of pursuing the Word of God to minister to problems of living. We encourage those who desire to help others to go to this source with confidence. No other way has such power for transformation.

Because of the importance of the Bible above all other sources of help, we do not attempt to give specific answers for specific problems. A specific system may shed some light and give some direction. But any specific plan may also stand in the way of going directly to the Lord and His Word. If a method of direction is spelled out, the counselor may use that rather than diligently pursuing the Word and seeking the face of the Lord on behalf of the counselee and his need.

Books utilizing a biblical approach to counseling can be helpful as long as they do not replace direct use of the Bible. Rather, they should elevate the use of the Bible and motivate a counselor to use the Word of God rather than the systems of men. Books that give examples of how the Bible is used during counseling demonstrate the effectiveness of using the Word. But a counselor should not attempt to copy those examples specifically, for each counselee and counseling relationship is unique. Instead, there should be a spontaneous flow of the mercy and truth of God. The counselor must go directly to the Word of God and to the Lord who will open the Word and make application.

PRAY FOR THE LEADING OF THE HOLY SPIRIT

The Lord has given both His Word and His Holy Spirit to enable the counselor and counselee to know and obey Him. Throughout Scripture, the Lord encourages His people to seek His wisdom and His will through prayer. In fact, pursuit of the Word and prayer go hand-in-hand as one seeks the mind of God.

My son, if you will receive my sayings,
And treasure my commandments within you,
Make your ear attentive to wisdom,
Incline your heart to understanding;
For if you cry for discernment,
Lift your voice for understanding;
If you seek her as silver,
And search for her as for hidden treasures;
Then you will discern the fear of the Lord,
And discover the knowledge of God.
For the Lord gives wisdom;
From His mouth come knowledge and understanding.
(Proverbs 2:1-6)

The Lord accomplishes much of His gracious will for His children through prayer. Through prayer, both the counselor and counselee may enter into the very presence of God to "receive mercy and . . . find grace to help in time of need" (Hebrews 4:16). The counselor will encourage the counselee to seek the Lord through prayer both during counseling and during the week.

The counselor will begin praying for the counselee some time before the actual counseling begins, both to intercede for the counselee and to present himself before God for cleansing so that he will be a clear channel of God's blessing, wisdom, truth, mercy, and grace. Much of what happens in biblical counseling is dependent upon what happens in prayer. Asking, seeking, and knocking with persistence and a ready ear are the ways Jesus gave to find help for others as well as for oneself. Faithfulness in prayer is the mark of a counselor who looks to God for change and growth and who continues to be sensitive to the working of the Spirit in a counselee's life.

In biblical counseling, conversation with a counselee must be based upon communication with God. Some problems seem to persist in spite of careful instruction. Only the Lord can reveal the root of a problem or the way out for a particular counselee. Such times of prayer are conferences with the Chief Counselor. The counselor is not just presenting the problem and asking God to do something; he is seeking to know how he might cooperate with God in bringing healing, restoration, reconciliation, and renewal.

A biblical counselor may follow much of the prayer life of Paul as he prayed for the early believers. Such prayers have been recorded and have great strength because they were inspired by God. Some of them may be found in Ephesians 1:17-19 and 3:16-19; Philippians 1:9-11; Colossians 1:9-12; and 2 Thessalonians 1:11-12. There are also many helpful books on prayer, but again the Bible must be the primary source for all that a counselor does and says.

Spiritual counseling is spiritual warfare. A biblical counselor cannot win with fleshly or man-made weapons, for he is ministering in the midst of a spiritual battle between the God of glory and the forces of evil.

> For our struggle is not against flesh and blood, but against the rulers, against the powers, against the world forces of this darkness, against the spiritual forces of wickedness in the heavenly places. (Ephesians 6:12)

The counselor must maintain and wear his armor, practice using his shield, and become an expert with his sword, which is the Word of God. His greatest and most significant activity occurs within his communication with God through reading the Word and praying.

PRESENT THE LORD'S WAY AS REVEALED BY THE WORD AND THE SPIRIT

Presenting the way of the Lord as revealed by the Word of God and the Holy Spirit includes both the manner of presentation and the content of conversation. The conversation of biblical counseling calls for a combination of mercy and truth and a balance of listening and speaking.

Because God desires to draw persons closer to Himself through love, biblical counseling must be given in love. Yet since God's love includes truth as well, biblical counseling should reflect that characteristic, too.

> Let not mercy and truth forsake thee: bind them about thy neck; write them upon the table of thine heart: So shalt thou find favour and good understanding in the sight of God and man. (Proverbs 3:3-4, KJV)

The Bible does not teach a methodology of merely reflecting a person's feelings, nor one of shallow sentimentality, nor one of autocratic severity. The Bible teaches, through countless illustrations and principles, that there must be a combination of mercy and truth.

Any counseling that lacks this combination will fall short of the Bible's standard.

Scripture is firm and unchanging in principle. The counseling process is not rigid, however. Jesus did not minister in an identical way to all individuals. He met each person where he was without lowering the standard. In so doing, Jesus revealed this balance of mercy and truth. In wisdom Jesus presented truth and justice in the manner most effective for each particular person. When the rich young ruler came to Jesus, Jesus ministered truth in mercy when He said that to follow God the young man would have to sell all he had. But without changing the standard, Jesus had a different message for Nicodemus: the need to be born again. If these messages had been reversed, there would not have been a perfect balance of mercy and truth because the spiritual sensitivity to the individual's need would have been missing.

COUNSELING MERCY AND TRUTH

A biblical counselor is called to be a vessel of God's mercy and a teacher of God's truth. Spiritual counseling is a creative process. God molds people with hands of love. Though truth requires change, God in His mercy never works more rapidly than an individual can tolerate at one time. The Lord is gentle and compassionate, and a spiritual counselor will want to reflect the Lord in the loving care of an individual. Within a safe environment of mercy and concern and with the sure Word of truth, a counselee may venture to learn, to change, and to grow.

As a counselor ministers according to the grace of God he will combine mercy and truth. If a counselor tends to stress mercy, he will need to be careful to balance mercy with teaching and exhorting according to truth. On the other hand, if he tends to stress exhortation, he will need to develop the quality of mercy.

As a spiritual counselor discerns areas of the counselee's life in which the Lord is working, he also needs to know what proportion of mercy and truth should characterize his exercise of ministry. Before Jesus raised Lazarus from the dead, He taught truth to Martha, wept with Mary, and urged Martha to a greater level of faith. In aptly joining mercy with truth, patience with exhortation, and listening with teaching, a counselor will need to rely continually upon the Holy Spirit for wisdom.

Mercy is extremely important in counseling. However, mercy exercised in the flesh may become mere sentimentality. Mercy not tempered by truth may take on the sufferings of others without leading them out of their suffering. When the suffering is internalized by a counselor through unbiblical mercy, the counselor may take on the hurt of the counselee and thereby become bitter and resentful along with the counselee. As soon as the counselor takes on the sinful feelings of a counselee (such as anger, bitterness, or hostility), he becomes part of the problem rather than part of the answer. Such feelings hinder the work of the Holy Spirit. Instead, a counselor should seek to maintain an attitude of kindness, mercy, and concern, undergirded by great faith in the character of God.

An individual needs truth to be set free from past bondages in thinking, feeling, and acting. Therefore, within the supportive relationship of mercy, a counselor will teach truth and may strongly urge a counselee to obey the truth. Paul continually ministered God's truth through exhortation, along with careful teaching and compassion. He wrote:

> Finally then, brethren, we request and exhort you in the Lord Jesus that, as you received from us instruction as to how you ought to walk and please God (just as you actually do walk), that you may excel still more. For you know what commandments we gave you by the authority of the Lord Jesus. (1 Thessalonians 4:1-2)

Then he continued with a particular subject of exhortation:

> For this is the will of God, your sanctification; that is, that you abstain from sexual immorality; that each of you know how to possess his own vessel in sanctification and honor, not in lustful passion, like the Gentiles who do not know God. (1 Thessalonians 4:3-5)

Paul did not fear hurting somebody's feelings when he saw that a direct word of exhortation was necessary. Yet that does not mean that the counselor should be insensitive. Much damage has been done through the exercise of exhortation that did not include mercy and instruction. Counselees may be turned off before they are ready to turn God's way. Exhortation without mercy, exercised in the flesh, may lead to severe dogmatism. Unbalanced exhortation may also reveal a critical attitude that will prevent effective counseling. A counselor who exhibits dogmatism, a critical attitude, and the tendency to snap out quick orders from the Bible merely adds to the condemnation and may even promote rebellion. On the other hand, when exhortation includes both mercy and careful instruction, an individual is encouraged to make right choices. His ability to choose to be responsible grows, and his dependence upon the Lord increases.

Each era struggles with the extremities of laxity and legalism. Earlier eras were characterized by legalism; now we are in an era characterized by laxity. What is needed today is a combination of mercy and truth based upon the Word of God.

Through exhibiting mercy and truth, the counselor can provide an environment for change and the direction for change. Much truth of Scripture is not at all threatening, but rather uplifting as it describes the mercy of God for the believer and other qualities of the character of God. But when the truth to be ministered calls for a change in thinking, feeling, or acting, a counselor should be careful to minister the right amount of corrective truth at the right time.

One way of reaching the right balance of truth and mercy is to match the amount of truth given to a counselee with the level of conviction that is necessary for change. Giving the counselee less truth than he really needs to hear may be useless. Yet giving him more truth than he can assimilate and obey may lead to discouragement and confusion. The counselor must be sensitive to the Holy Spirit in this matter, for only the Holy Spirit knows the right truth to minister at a particular time to a particular person to encourage faith, responsibility, and love for God.

One counselee may receive direct instruction and be motivated to change. But another counselee may need encouragement to be motivated. Often a person who has lived with a great deal of criticism receives teaching best when it is in terms of what he is already doing right. If the counselor expresses positive encouragement, the counselee may be motivated to continue in that good direction. For some people the failures and the negatives loom large on their horizon when in actuality they may be doing many things the way God would desire.

Encouragement may be called for rather than, or in addition to, correction. If a person understands what he is doing correctly, he will be encouraged to continue in the right direction and be more open to further instruction. The counselor may stimulate an individual to continue a path of action or a new thought pattern. He may point out certain good actions or situations arising from the new patterns to motivate the counselee to continue doing things God's way. Encouragement may sometimes be general but at other times be quite specific. The general prompting of the person to discover God's will and to follow His ways is a constant attitude and activity of the counselor. Then the specific urging may be reserved for encouraging the counselee to take important actions he hesitates to begin.

The counseling process begins at the foot of the cross. The spiritual counselor who understands his own flesh and his own need to depend on the Lord will have mercy and compassion for the counselee and will not stand in judgment. Though a spiritual counselor cannot condone sin, as he recognizes the hurt and the unfulfilled needs of the person he is counseling, he will desire to bring that person to the place of forgiveness, healing, encouragement, and faith.

> For God did not send the Son into the world to judge the world; but that the world should be saved through Him. (John 3:17)

> My brethren, if any among you strays from the truth, and one turns him back; let him know that he who turns a sinner from the error of his way will save his soul from death, and will cover a multitude of sins. (James 5:19-20)

A biblical counselor looks beyond the sin to the hurt and the expression of the flesh trying to meet its own needs. He sees a person in need of mercy, but he also knows that healing and transformation come only through repentance and forgiveness, assisted by instruction and encouragement.

An excellent example of truth and mercy extended to an individual without the condoning of sin can be seen in John 8:1-11. When the scribes and Pharisees brought to Jesus a woman who had been caught in the act of adultery, they demanded a response in order to trick Him. But Jesus demonstrated the love of God, which transforms lives. He gave everyone the opportunity to examine his own life in the light of God's law when He said, "He who is without sin among you, let him be the first to throw a stone at her." Then as Jesus wrote on the ground, "they began to go out one by one, beginning with the older ones, and He was left alone, and the woman, where she had been, in the midst." Jesus gave each person

the occasion to examine his own life so that each might be convicted
in his own conscience. During this time the woman's conscience
surely spoke to her. She knew she was guilty and evidently confessed her sin within her own heart, for Jesus said to her, "Neither do
I condemn you; go your way; from now on sin no more."

Jesus gave the woman both mercy and truth, for though He did
not condemn her He did admonish her to change her behavior. Thus
she went away forgiven and having made a valid choice for change.
Without departing from the truth or from the Father's standard of
righteousness, Jesus was caring, forgiving, and strengthening in His
response to her. He neither condoned nor condemned. He loved and
cared enough to give the amount of truth that could be received
within the context of love.

A counselor needs to be faithful to the whole counsel of God. If
he gives the counselee only the words that are easy and acceptable,
the counselee may remain weak and spiritually stagnant. The
counselor should remember that without the recognition of our own
sins, there is no Good News of God's saving grace. God's Word will
not return without accomplishing something. Even Jesus found that
many rejected His words. But triumph eventually followed. Paul
wrote:

> But thanks be to God, who always leads us in His triumph in Christ,
> and manifests through us the sweet aroma of the knowledge of Him in
> every place. For we are a fragrance of Christ to God among those who
> are being saved and among those who are perishing; to the one an
> aroma from death to death, to the other an aroma from life to life. And
> who is adequate for these things? (2 Corinthians 2:14-16)

Victory in counseling comes through being faithful to God and to
His Word. It does not come through craving immediate external
results. Faithful is the counselor who speaks "in Christ in the sight of
God" (2 Corinthians 2:17).

The comfort of mercy. Sometimes when a person has experienced
loss or when he is going through difficult trials, the counselor's work
is not necessarily to instruct, but rather to comfort and particularly to
bring the comfort of the Lord.

> Blessed be the God and Father of our Lord Jesus Christ, the Father of
> mercies and God of all comfort; who comforts us in all our affliction so
> that we may be able to comfort those who are in any affliction with the

comfort with which we ourselves are comforted by God. (2 Corinthians 1:3-4)

Comfort from God will ease grief and bring strength and hope. Often the counselor who has experienced similar loss or trials will be able to give greater comfort than the counselor who has not yet lived through the experience. Nevertheless, nearly every Christian has encountered enough losses and problems of one sort or another to have discovered the comfort only God can give. Such comfort will lead to peace and healing and renewed strength. But a counselor should avoid commiserating with a person who has chosen to remain in grief rather than to move toward receiving God's comfort and life. God uses His comfort to accomplish growth, change, and new strength in an individual rather than just for the purpose of making him feel better.

When a Christian goes through a time of great change or difficult adjustment in life he may need a fellow believer to go through it with him. These times include such life adjustments as the death of a loved one, divorce, loss of health, loss of a job, and certain types of family problems. In such situations the counselor helps mainly by listening, identifying with the loss, and giving emotional and especially spiritual support. Moreover, the counselor sensitively offers hope and encouragement for the future. He attempts to bring the focus of the eyes upon Jesus and the eternal promises of the Bible. This can only be done gently and in faith. It is like applying oil to the wound. If a person tries to push hope and faith without identifying with compassion and love, he may cause the wound to smart, as though he had applied vinegar instead of oil.

During times of loss, disappointment, and grief the counselor needs to be patient with the person, who may be expressing angry feelings toward God. Through love, patience, and encouragement a counselor can lead such a person to a more accurate consideration of God and a greater understanding of His character and His comfort. Rather than condemning the sufferer for expressing negative thoughts, a wise counselor will silently pray for the hurt individual, steadfastly love him, and gently lead him into the ways of the Lord.

Listening for truth in mercy. A biblical counselor listens to love, learn, and lead. He listens with mercy to identify with the counselee, to understand what he is experiencing, and to express the love and concern of God. Such listening is more than empathic listening, however. It is not just for the counselee to "get it all out" so that he will somehow be relieved, but rather for the counselee to learn in an environment of God's love. In identifying with the counselee, the biblical counselor receives the person just as he is and recognizes that no matter what his present condition the Lord loves him. God loves every person in spite of his sin, but He loves him too much to leave him the way he is. God came to save and sanctify sinners, not just to accept them and let them live forever in misery.

Responsive listening involves the heart, mind, eyes, and body, as well as the ears. It is an attitude that can originate from a loving heart and can be developed through daily practice. Just by listening, a counselor can communicate respect, concern, and love. As he listens to the words being spoken by the counselee he is, at the same time, considering God's great love and concern for the one who is speaking.

The response of the counselor is often the loudest statement he makes. Quite often a counselee watches the facial expressions of a counselor to check whether or not it is safe to continue sharing. Sometimes a counselee will test the response of the counselor over a period of time before he decides to discuss what is really on his heart. For instance, when someone confesses some lurid sin, a reaction of righteous indignation, shock, or morbid curiosity would not establish a good counseling atmosphere. On the other hand, a response of concern for the spiritual welfare of the counselee and of patience and meekness (quiet strength without a hint of superiority) can establish a safe place for spiritual transformation.

The counselor can hold certain truths in mind while a counselee is confessing devastating sin: What is being said right now is of crucial importance to this individual. God loves him and has a way out of this destruction. A confession like this is not strange to God's ears, though He grieves for him and desires to minister mercy, grace, forgiveness, and truth to transform the counselee. Such confession prepares a person to repent and turn from the sin to the Lord and His way. The person has come to the counselor for help and needs someone who can listen without fear and who can point to God's way out of the problems.

The emotional response of listening in mercy prepares the climate for truth, and intelligent listening helps the counselor determine what areas of truth need to be explored or emphasized. The Bible speaks of the value of listening for truth:

> He who gives an answer before he hears,
> It is folly and shame to him
> (Proverbs 18:13)

Through thoughtful listening the counselor can gain necessary information and provide an objective perspective.

Active, intelligent listening enables a counselor to find out information and gain clarity in areas of confusion. However, the process of listening in the counseling setting is often like a game of hide and seek, because guilt, bitterness, and unforgiveness may be concealed beneath the besetting problem. Hurt may be buried beneath anger. Hostility may be lurking behind fear. Besides unintentional deception, there may be intentional deception and withholding of information.

In one study of patients receiving psychotherapy, it was discovered that "forty percent of [the patients] admitted that they were withholding information from their therapists."[1] At a day-long symposium at Columbia University, "the psychoanalytic relationship was seen as a prime example of how human communication can depend on lies."[2] Though any counseling relationship should be an honest one, many are not. Besides withholding information and deliberately lying, people communicate what they believe to be true only as they see a situation, which is from a limited and biased position. A counselor therefore cannot always depend upon receiving accurate information from a counselee. Proverbs 18:17 says:

> The first to plead his case seems just,
> Until another comes and examines him.

The counselor must be cautious in listening to a person's explanations or descriptions of situations.

Discriminating listening involves careful attention and pertinent questions.

> The mind of the prudent acquires knowledge,
> And the ear of the wise seeks knowledge.
> (Proverbs 18:15)

1. Lori B. Andrews, "What People Don't Tell Therapists," *Psychology Today,* September 1982, p. 16.
2. Kenneth Woodward, "Lying All the Way to the Truth," *Psychology Today,* November 1982, p. 20.

Questions of the *what, how, when, where,* and *to what extent* variety are generally more helpful than those asking *why.* Discretion is imperative in asking *why* questions. Although in some instances they may elicit valuable information, they more often lead to self-justification and rationalization, rather than promote new ways of thinking and acting. Clarity can more often be seen in what a person did or plans to do. Nathan did not ask David why he committed adultery with Bathsheba and murdered Uriah the Hittite. Instead he confronted him with what he did. On the other hand, when Samuel asked Saul, "What meaneth the bleating of the sheep?" Saul offered a rationalization and justification for his sin.

Whether a counselor understands what the individual is really saying or whether he just thinks he understands is an area of concern that can be dealt with through questions of clarification and even through attempting to restate what the counselee has said. In trying to communicate a feeling or deep inner response to a situation or a complex network of circumstances, a counselee is limited to the vocabulary of ordinary language. To further compound the problem, words carry varying emotional overtones and subtle variations of meaning. There is a strong temptation for a counselor to act as though he understands when he may not have the kind of comprehension required. A good listener will check to see if he is grasping what is meant as well as what is being said. The counselor will also need to rely on the Lord to bring understanding, because words cannot fully communicate what a person is experiencing. Some people speak in such poetic terms that the counselor has to interpret what is being said, and others speak with such ordinary language that much is left unsaid.

Questions stimulating clear thinking and perception can be extremely beneficial in opening ways of thinking and behaving according to God's truth. Sometimes a counselor may attempt to aid a counselee by asking such questions as: "Did you mean to say that . . . ?" This helps the counselee notice what comments or innuendoes are slipping past his lips. Such attention also tends to make the counselee more responsible for what he says. Quite often people fall into a pattern of letting hurtful remarks slip out without the least sense of concern. By providing focus through questions, a counselor can also prevent a certain amount of rambling and repetition. Rather than just going on and on or talking in circles, the conversation can move in the direction of restoration, change, or a new course of action.

Questions of clarification are useful to both the counselor and counselee. Both need a clear focus; both need discernment and wisdom. As a counselor listens objectively and asks questions, the counselee may begin to see the nature of his problem more clearly and may even discover answers. Furthermore, when a counselor has listened and sought to understand, the counselee is more receptive to consider what the counselor says.

TEACHING AND LEARNING FOR CHANGE

As important as listening is within the counseling context, listening alone is usually not enough. Careful instruction and guidance through practical application of biblical principles are often necessary for change. Spiritual counseling is much like private Bible instruction. Rather than teaching the biblical principles to a group, however, the counselor tailors the instruction to meet the needs of the individual. Biblical counseling involves the whole counsel of God, because only God knows what is really needed at the moment as well as in the future. Both a working knowledge of Scripture and the active presence of the Holy Spirit are essential in every counseling conversation. Not only the specific teachings, but also the manner of instruction, will be personalized.

Teaching principles from the Word of God will be interwoven throughout a counseling conversation. Since all believers need to learn how to live more effectively according to God's design, practical suggestions as to how and what to change should grow out of the biblical principles which apply to the situation. Also, a counselor who has faced similar challenges in life can not only point toward the goal but also can point out chuckholes to avoid and the sudden curves that are coming. Otherwise the counselee will think that no one else has ever failed.

Since the Holy Spirit speaks effectively through the Bible, the spiritual counselor will rely on the Bible as his primary source book. Paul's wise advice to Timothy applies directly to biblical counseling:

> And the Lord's bond-servant must not be quarrelsome, but be kind to all, able to teach, patient when wronged, with gentleness correcting

those who are in opposition; if perhaps God may grant them repentance leading to the knowledge of the truth, and they may come to their
senses and escape from the snare of the devil, having been held captive
by him to do his will. (2 Timothy 2:24-26)

I solemnly charge you in the presence of God and of Christ Jesus, who
is to judge the living and the dead, and by His appearing and His
kingdom: preach the word; be ready in season and out of season;
reprove, rebuke, exhort, with great patience and instruction. (2
Timothy 4:1-2)

Note the manner of instruction and the source of instruction. The
teaching is based on the Word of God, includes correction and
encouragement, and is given in kindness and patience with great
care. Correction can only be accomplished effectively in love with
great respect for the individual. When rebuke is necessary, there
needs to be careful instruction as to how one might change or do
things differently.

Whenever the Lord points out error, He also shows the right
way. Rather than condemnation there is hope and help for change.
Often correction can be given as an alternative plan of action or
behavior. When someone truly sees that choices are available and
recognizes that certain alternatives agree with God's will for him, he
will not see such correction as criticism, but rather as hope.

Each Christian is in the process of being recreated. He is
vulnerable and he is precious. Therefore, the counselor should seek
God's wisdom in determining which positive actions need to be
encouraged and which errors call for attention. The obvious errors
may not be the first ones the Lord will correct. In fact, with some
counselees certain errors may need to be overlooked until the
counselees have the security of God's goodness and grace. The Lord
bore the Israelites on eagle's wings before He gave them the law.
Jesus died for us while we were still sinners. Mercy often precedes
precepts and principles.

As a counselee becomes a willing learner, he is more and more
open to see possiblities for change and growth. He will begin to pay
attention to the Lord and also to his own actions and words. He will
check them with Scripture to see if he is thinking and acting
according to the life of Jesus in him or according to the ways of the
flesh. Within the security of the love of God and within the security

of a counselor who will not condemn, a counselee will be free to pay attention to what he is doing, without fear, so that he can submit every area of his life to the Lord for transformation. The Pharisees were too proud to learn. They already considered themselves to be experts and were not open to correction or change. They defended their own righteousness to the point of persecuting and crucifying Jesus. Some in the crowds were too fearful to hear truth because they feared condemnation. Fear and pride alike can prevent learning, and both come from the flesh.

Finally, a counselee must learn biblical principles by doing them. Just learning facts in the head or enjoying insight will not accomplish much unless there is action. Jesus said that those who hear and do the will of God are wise. James encourages doing as well as hearing. Therefore, a counselor will encourage a counselee to put into active practice what he is learning.

As a counselee learns to look to Jesus and be yoked to Him, he can yield himself to the inner work Jesus desires to perform. Jesus does the major work of transformation, while the believer cooperates and yields by working out whatever Jesus is working within.

PART 3

Change Through God's Love

11

Receiving and Giving Love

God's love is the primary motivation for growth and change. Receiving God's love and following the "great commandment" of Matthew 22:36 are major goals in biblical counseling. They will bring about transformation in any problems of living that can be touched by talk therapy.

RECEIVING GOD'S LOVE

In counseling the order of love must be observed: God loved first. The love of God precedes the admonition to love God. If we require another person to love God without believing or receiving love from God, the person may fall into the flesh, trying to love God so that God will love him. Thus, the emphasis in counseling is God's love. God's love, given in a multitude of ways and dramatically demonstrated through the sacrifice of Christ, penetrates the darkness of unbelief. Believing God is the opposite of the response of unbelief that originated in the Garden and separates people from God. God's love, based on truth and righteousness, provides the way into relationship.

God knows us through and through and still loves us. His love is not sentimental or changeable, but dependable and faithful. When one is well-loved by God and others and responds to that love by believing and loving, he is more likely to follow the Spirit than to live according to the flesh.

Believing and receiving the love of God are vital for living the Christian life. As obvious as this sounds, many Christians do not consistently experience the ongoing, never-changing love of God. They try to be good Christians and become discouraged with themselves, not realizing that they need to be more aware of His love. In short, they need to know God better and believe His Word.

In teaching the love of God, the counselor will stress those aspects of God's character that the counselee needs to hear. Since His love undergirds, amplifies, and modifies every quality of His character, teaching about His love will include teaching about His sovereignty, power, truth, holiness, faithfulness, wisdom, justice, righteousness, grace, mercy, forgiveness, patience, and tenderness. The counselee needs to learn about and to experience God's love through faith.

Many who suffer from a distorted concept of God do not experience His grace. Some attempt to earn His love, or they look within themselves and see that they do not deserve His love. They do not realize that they are loved by grace, not by merit—on the basis of the cross of Jesus rather than by their own personal righteousness. Others have blamed God or other people for so long that they demand evidence of God's love in their circumstances and in their feelings. They have become judges of God, and though they fear His power, they do not believe He can be trusted. Such people live in the bondage of unbelief and have become gods unto themselves.

Others equate love with having their own way, which is another form of self as god. They do not see that God's love will not violate His will, which is always good and perfect (no matter how circumstances may look). No one can understand the love of God by looking at himself or at his circumstances. The most effective way of seeing and believing God's love is to look at the cross of Christ.

> For while we were still helpless, at the right time Christ died for the ungodly. For one will hardly die for a righteous man; though perhaps for the good man someone would dare even to die. But God demonstrates His own love toward us, in that while we were yet sinners, Christ died for us. (Romans 5:6-8)

God's love is so tremendously giving that He was willing to pay the full price for the sins of mankind in order to extend and express His love and His life to humanity.

Love is the most important truth for a Christian, and yet the word *love* has been distorted and watered down. Therefore, a Christian needs to look constantly at love in reference to the Bible and to the revelation of God's love demonstrated through Jesus. Biblical love is far from sentimentalism. It is powerful and tender at the same time. It is a love that will never depart from the truth or from justice and righteousness. The most complete description in the Bible of love is found in 1 Corinthians 13:

> Love is patient, love is kind, and is not jealous; love does not brag and is not arrogant, does not act unbecomingly; it does not seek its own, is not provoked, does not take into account a wrong suffered, does not rejoice in unrighteousness, but rejoices with the truth; bears all things, believes all things, hopes all things, endures all things. Love never fails. . . . But now abide faith, hope, love, these three; but the greatest of these is love. (1 Corinthians 13:4-8, 13)

This description of love fits Jesus more than anyone else; however, the life of the Holy Spirit indwelling a counselor has this same kind of love. And this is the love on which the biblical counselor must continually draw. All counseling must fit this description of love as much as possible, for this kind of love gives life to the counselee. As such love is given to the counselee by the Lord and also by the counselor, and as such love is received by the counselee, transformation comes, and the counselee grows emotionally and spiritually in such a way as to reflect the Lord and to meet the challenges of life.

Because the love of God is such an essential and profound aspect of the Christian life, the counselor will also spend much time praying for the counselee to know, believe, and receive the love of God. He may turn to Paul's prayer for the Ephesians:

> For this reason, I bow my knees before the Father, from whom every family in heaven and on earth derives its name, that He would grant you, according to the riches of His glory, to be strengthened with power through His Spirit in the inner man; so that Christ may dwell in your hearts through faith; and that you, being rooted and grounded in love, may be able to comprehend with all the saints what is the breadth and length and height and depth, and to know the love of Christ which surpasses knowledge, that you may be filled up to all the fulness of God. (Ephesians 3:14-19)

Paul knew that when such love is received by a Christian the Holy Spirit is able to accomplish great things through that individual. Thus he ends his prayer by saying,

> Now to Him who is able to do exceeding abundantly beyond all that we ask or think, according to the power that works within us, to Him be the glory in the church and in Christ Jesus to all generations forever and ever. Amen. (Ephesians 3:20-21)

God's love flowed through the cross of Christ so that mankind could reenter the relationship He had intended and so that He could enter into a person's life to give that person the qualities of His character: holiness, righteousness, truth, faith, moral responsibility, love, forgiveness, and mercy. Although God maintains His own supremacy and power, He operates His kingdom and His power through the lives of His children who have chosen to receive Him. An understanding of the character of God is just the beginning movement in knowing Him, experiencing His love and His life, becoming a vessel for His character, and growing into His likeness. Only God's love could reverse the results of the Fall and enable people to believe Him, act responsibly according to faith in Him, and love God in obedience.

FOLLOWING THE GREAT COMMANDMENT

Because the love relationship with God is the essence of Christianity, love for God is the most essential response. Love for God is the motivating force for living according to God's will. Therefore, the "great commandment" is central to biblical counseling.

> The foremost is, "Hear, O Israel; The Lord our God is One Lord; and you shall love the Lord your God with all your heart, and with all your soul, and with all your mind, and with all your strength." The second is this, "You shall love your neighbor as yourself." There is no other commandment greater than these. (Mark 12:29-31)

Along with John 3:16, the "great commandment" is at the core of Christianity. It defines the love relationship from which the abundant life flows.

LOVING GOD

The "great commandment" is founded first of all on God's love for mankind. The apostle John wrote, "In this is love, not that we loved God, but that He loved us and sent His Son to be the propitiation for our sins" (1 John 4:10). The commandment to love God sets forth the believer's response to the love of God. The most basic and fundamental choice of change for the Christian is to actively respond to God's love by believing His love and by loving God with every aspect of his being, including thoughts, emotions, and actions. Humans were created for a love relationship with God and to be channels of love to one another. Until one moves in this relationship he will be out of harmony with life itself.

Loving God is more than just an emotional response of feeling love. It is an activity involving all of one's mind, will, heart, and strength, and therefore is to be practiced at all times. In discussing ways in which a person may love God, the counselor will first of all stress the importance of believing and trusting God. The writer to the Hebrews said: "And without faith it is impossible to please Him, for he who comes to God must believe that He is, and that He is a rewarder of those who seek Him" (Hebrews 11:6). Love for God is demonstrated through willing obedience to His will. God's love is the very source of life and is the divine power that enables a believer to live as God designed him to live—in wisdom, in submission to God, in humility, in power, in faith, in hope, and in love.

Within this very response comes a giving of the self. Jesus gave His life for each believer because of love. Therefore, as a response to that love, the believer gives himself to God.

> I urge you therefore, brethren, by the mercies of God, to present your bodies a living and holy sacrifice, acceptable to God, which is your spiritual service of worship. And do not be conformed to this world, but be transformed by the renewing of your mind, that you may prove what the will of God is, that which is good and acceptable and perfect. (Romans 12:1-2)

Such giving and receiving brings about transformation. As the believer yields himself to the Holy Spirit, he becomes more and more like Jesus. Jesus put it this way:

If any one wishes to come after Me, let him deny himself, and take up his cross, and follow Me. For whoever wishes to save his life shall lose it; but whoever loses his life for My sake shall find it. (Matthew 16:24-25)

Love for God may also be expressed through honoring Him as God and worshiping Him exclusively. In honoring Him as God, one puts his trust more in God than in any other person, object, or system of ideas. Worship of God also supplants lesser desires or puts them into proper perspective. Honoring God implies that He is a good God and that His character is fully righteous, holy, just, and kind. God is thus given credit for all goodness, perfection, and beauty.

Another practical way of loving God is thanking Him. Again, the practice honors Him as the source of all goodness. A counselee could begin a list of all for which he can be thankful. Such attention to gratitude brings a holy perspective to difficult, negative circumstances. Those Christians who live close to the Lord will in the midst of grief express an overflowing gratitude to the Lord, not for the cause of the grief but for the precious presence of God and for all the good He has brought into their lives.

A most basic way of loving God is abiding in Him, depending on Him as the source for life and ministry, and choosing not to act independently from Him. To ignore the life of God within the believer is to do Him great injustice, but to live in relationship to His indwelling presence is to love Him. Such dependence on the Lord implies the kind of humility that says, "Without Him I can do nothing, but with Him I can do His will." The believer who has that attitude truly gives all credit and glory to God rather than taking credit for himself.

As a counselor teaches these principles for loving God, he will be able to tailor them to the areas of need in the counselee. Although some counselees act independently because of a strong personality, others do so because they do not understand the principles of walking after the Spirit in a dependent relationship with the Father. Furthermore, learning to live in dependency on the Lord is a gradual process that develops with experience.

The most important way some counselees can love God is to believe His love even when their feelings do not confirm that love. Feelings do not always agree with the truth of God's constant love.

Therefore, a counselor may suggest that remembering the fact of God's love and responding to that truth (whether it is felt or not) will strengthen the person's ability both to receive God's love and to love Him in return. Often a clear explanation of how God's Word applies to the person's problem demonstrates God's loving concern and help. Another way for the counselee to confirm the love relationship is for him to tell other people about the faithfulness, kindness, and love of God in his own life. In fact, a counselor may ask, "In what ways has God shown His love to you this week?"

Finally, trusting and obeying God are vital signs of loving God. Obedience to God's Word is of great importance. However, some people obey in order to earn the love of God and others. True obedience is actually the result of the love relationship. Jesus said, "He who has My commandments, and keeps them, he it is who loves Me; and he who loves Me shall be loved by My Father, and I will love him, and will disclose Myself to him" (John 14:21). Although God loved first, a Christian's response of obedience keeps the flow of love going. God never stops loving, but obedience enables an individual to continue to receive God's love. Therefore, obedience is an act of love directed toward God.

A counselor will encourage obedience on the basis of God's love and on the basis of the truth that God's principles are for an individual's good. All of God's law is good. His law is righteous and just. That is why Jesus concluded the "great commandment," to love God, and the "second," to love one's neighbor, with the words: "On these two commandments depend the whole Law and the Prophets" (Matthew 22:40). All goodness and righteousness proceed from God's love and flow through an individual's love for God and others. Love is the motivation for obedience to God, and obedience to God is an act of love.

LOVING NEIGHBOR

One of the most visible expressions of loving God is loving people. The apostle John noted that one could not claim to love God if he did not love his fellow man as well.

We love, because He first loved us. If some one says, "I love God," and hates his brother, he is a liar; for the one who does not love his brother whom he has seen, cannot love God whom he has not seen. And this

commandment we have from Him, that the one who loves God should
love his brother also. (1 John 4:19-21)

Jesus placed the importance of loving our neighbor right next to the
commandment to love God.

God's love enables Christians to love one another even in
difficult circumstances. That love does not come from mere human
resources, but from God Himself as He is indwelling and loving the
believer. John wrote:

> And we have come to know and have believed the love which God has
> for us. God is love, and the one who abides in love abides in God, and
> God abides in him. By this, love is perfected in us. (1 John 4:16-17)

Paul also had much to say about Christians loving one another.

> And so, as those who have been chosen of God, holy and beloved, put
> on a heart of compassion, kindness, humility, gentleness and patience;
> bearing with one another, and forgiving each other, whoever has a
> complaint against any one; just as the Lord forgave you, so also should
> you. And beyond all these things put on love, which is the perfect bond
> of unity. (Colossians 3:12-14)

Note that Paul first reminded the believers of their position in
relationship to God as "chosen of God, holy and beloved" before he
described the way they were to love one another.

In the Body of Christ counselees may learn new ways of loving
as Jesus commanded, "Love one another, just as I have loved you"
(John 15:12). Jesus' love was not passive. He taught and healed many,
and He took upon Himself the judgment for our sin when He died
on the cross. Love in action was also stressed by James when he
called Christians to act according to their faith, and thus to love with
action:

> If a brother or sister is without clothing and in need of daily food, and
> one of you says to them, "Go in peace, be warmed and be filled," and
> yet you do not give them what is necessary for their body, what use is
> that? (James 2:15-16)

Loving one's neighbor does not necessarily mean to feel affection or
sympathy for him. When Jesus told the story of the Samaritan as an

example of loving one's neighbor, he mentioned the Samaritan's concern for the wellbeing of the man beaten by robbers and the Samaritan's practical assistance of the man. The Samaritan put the other person's welfare above his own and went out of his way to see that the person's needs were met. And yet Jesus did not make any mention of affectionate feelings the Samaritan might have had.

Another way Jesus taught the concept of loving neighbor as self was through the Golden Rule:

> Therefore, whatever you want others to do for you, do so for them, for this is the Law and the Prophets. (Matthew 7:12)

Jesus was not only teaching people how to live in a socially responsible way; He was teaching them that happiness is a by-product of obeying God. A fascinating study on the principle of the Golden Rule was conducted by Bernard Rimland, director of the Institute for Child Behavior Research. Rimland found that "the happiest people are those who help others." Each person involved in the study was asked to list ten people he knew best and to label them as happy or not happy. Then they were to go through the list again and label each one as selfish or unselfish, using the following definition of selfishness:

> A stable tendency to devote one's time and resources to one's own interests and welfare—an unwillingness to inconvenience one's self for others.[1]

In categorizing the results, Rimland found that all of the people labeled *happy* were also labeled *unselfish*. He wrote that those "whose activities are devoted to *bringing themselves happiness* . . . are far less likely to be happy than those whose efforts are devoted to making others happy" (emphasis his). Rimland concluded: "Do unto others as you would have them do unto you."[2]

As a counselee chooses to love God through faith and obedience and as he chooses to love others through active, other-oriented living, he will not only find solutions to problems of relationship, but will find the fruit of the Spirit in greater abundance. If he evaluates his actions in terms of loving God and neighbor and in terms of

1. Bernard Rimland, "The Altruism Paradox," *Psychological Reports* 51 (1982): 521.
2. Ibid., p. 522.

obeying Jesus within the context of His love, he will certainly find opportunities for growth. Scripture provides the basic necessities for living a godly life of trust and obedience according to the love of God. Therefore, the "how to" of Scripture and the "how to" of counseling are the same: one must live in relationship to the God of love and must put the "great and foremost commandment" (Matthew 22:38) into action.

The focus of all counseling must be this profound relationship of love. Every problem can be met through a greater realization of God's love and through responding to His love. As two believers come together to seek God's solutions to problems, they will be examining thoughts, emotions, and actions in the context of God's love and God's Word. They will look at these in terms of creation—which includes the spiritual nature of man, the uniqueness of each person, and free will. They will look at these in terms of how the counselee may be reacting according to the old order, as though he is still separated from God, and therefore is acting out of unbelief, misdirected hope, or self-love. And they will look at these in terms of restoration—new life provided through the death and resurrection of Jesus, the indwelling Holy Spirit, and the Word of God. But above all and through all, they will look at thoughts, emotions, and actions in terms of relationship: God's love and the "great and foremost commandment."

12

Struggle of Love

The primary struggle, which began in the Garden and continues even after a person becomes a Christian, is the struggle of love. God created mankind to live in a love relationship with Himself, but when Adam and Eve chose to act independently they moved themselves out of the love relationship and became their own gods. In the separated condition, people develop an autonomous self that attempts to meet its own needs and desires apart from the life of God. It is that same self that tends, in a multitude of subtle ways, to love itself more than God and neighbor.

THE CONFLICT IN MAN OVER LOVE

Jesus thoroughly understood this struggle, as He showed when He answered the question about which commandment was the greatest:

> The foremost is, "Hear, O Israel; The Lord our God is One Lord; and you shall love the Lord your God with all your heart, and with all your soul, and with all your mind, and with all your strength." (Mark 12:29)

Love for God is of utmost significance because whom or what a person loves most becomes a god to him. Notice how Jesus combined the statement, "The Lord our God is One Lord," with the statement, "You shall love the Lord your God." Whatever is loved most has the central position in life. If God is loved most, He is in the central position. But if self is loved most, self is elevated to the place only God should occupy. The moment one puts his own will above God's will, he is loving himself more than God. Whenever a person puts his own desires above God's commandment, he is acting as his own god rather than submitting to the one true God.

Every problem becomes a temptation to love self more than God, but with every temptation, God gives the choice and the ability to move in relationship to Him. His love is there to enable us to meet the problem and overcome the temptation. Our choice is to love ourselves and do our own will through our own effort or to love God and do His will through His enabling.

Along with the inborn struggle between loving God and loving self, there is much encouragement from the world to love self. Because of the heavy influence of secular humanistic psychology, many people have become convinced that the source of their problems is that they do not love themselves enough. They believe that if they are to overcome the problems of living they must learn to love themselves.

Similarly, although Jesus taught His disciples to love God and others through thoughts, emotions, and actions consistent with God's love, many today espouse the teachings of self-love, self-esteem, and self-worth. They believe problems in their lives are the result of their having a low self-image. The antidote they provide is one of thinking and acting in such a way as to feel good about oneself. But the focus of Scripture has always been other-oriented rather than self-oriented, and it is far more accurate to say that one of the main roots of depression and other emotional and behavioral problems is self-preoccupation rather than lack of self-esteem.

Yet in spite of the fact that Scripture is other-oriented, even many Christian books are fanning the flames of self-centeredness. (This theme of self love is of recent vintage in the church. Though the cult of self-worship can be said to have originated in the Garden of Eden, it has only been in the past thirty years that we have had the time and money to be so self centered.) And on the heels of this self-centeredness has come a self-centered gospel sanctified by Scripture and saturated with self-love. John Piper says sadly, "Today the first and greatest commandment is 'Thou shalt love thyself.' " He rightly complains that today the "ultimate sin is no longer the failure to honor God and thank Him but the failure to esteem oneself."[1]

1. John Piper, "Is Self-Love Biblical?" *Christianity Today*, 12 August 1977, p. 6.

David Myers, in his book *The Inflated Self,* points out how research has revealed a self-serving bias in man.

Time and again experiments have revealed that people tend to attribute positive behaviors to themselves and negative behaviors to external factors, enabling them to take credit for their good acts and to deny responsibility for their bad acts.[2]

In experiments that required individuals to cooperate to accomplish a task, most individuals took the credit for successes and blamed their partners for the failures. The same pattern of blame and credit occurred when teams were told they had succeeded even when they did not or when teams were told that they had failed even though they had succeeded.[3] The results of these experiments agreed with the truth of Proverbs:

> All the ways of a man are clean in his own sight,
> But the Lord weighs the motives.
>
> (Proverbs 16:2)

Though many would claim that people need ego boosting, Myers's research led him to conclude that "Preachers who deliver ego-boosting pep talks to audiences who are supposedly plagued with miserable self images are preaching to a problem that seldom exists."[4]

This preoccupation with self has historic implications. Edward Stainbrook, nationally known as an expert on human behavior, believes that "self preoccupation is jeopardizing America's future" and that the vast amount of depression in our society is due to this self-preoccupation.[5] Psychiatrist Heinz Kohut says that narcissism is "the leading illness of our time."[6] Paul said that the mark of the last days would be self-love (2 Timothy 3:2).

Unfortunately, the main thrust of psychological counseling is toward self-enhancement rather than self-denial, toward self-love rather than self-sacrifice. The biblical counselor must recognize the

---

2. David G. Myers, *The Inflated Self* (New York: Seabury, 1980), p. 20.
3. Ibid., pp. 25-26.
4. Ibid., p. 24.
5. Edward Stainbrook, quoted by Lloyd Shearer, "Intelligence Report," *Parade Magazine,* 25 November 1979, p. 6.
6. Heinz Kohut, quoted by Lois Timnick, "Rift May Threaten Freudian Theory," *Los Angeles Times,* 27 October 1979, section 1-A, p. 1.

fallen nature of mankind from the Garden of Eden onward and the pull of the flesh even after the cross of Christ. Self-love is an appealing message, especially to the flesh, and denying self is anathema to the flesh. As a result, the particular motives, ambitions, and attitudes of a person are often the result of the fallen nature or the flesh. A commentator on a new twenty-year study of Americans says:

> It seems to me that the "new investment in self-expression and self-fulfillment"—barring war, famine, or a full-scale economic depression—is firmly entrenched in American psychic life.[7]

The concept of self-love is probably one of the most serious areas of misunderstanding and misapplication of Scripture in the church today. Misministering self-acceptance, self-esteem, self-worth, and self-love will only amplify the lower tendencies of the flesh and end up in self-worship. Someone once wisely said, "It is not who we are but Whose we are." I am accepted in Christ; I am esteemed in Christ; I am of worth in Christ. But when the *who* is detached from the *Whose*, one is out of the Spirit and into self.

SELF-LOVE NOT A SCRIPTURAL GOAL

Self-love is not taught as a positive goal in Scripture. Jesus said that the mark of the true disciple is self-denial (Mark 8:34). Paul Vitz notes the danger of self and pride:

> The relentless and single-minded search for and glorification of the self is at direct cross purposes with the Christian injunction to *lose* thyself. Certainly Jesus Christ neither lived nor advocated a life that would qualify by today's standards as "self-actualized." For the Christian the self is the problem, not the potential paradise. Understanding this problem involves an awareness of sin, especially the sin of pride; correcting this condition requires the practice of such un-self-actualized states as contrition and penitence, humility, obedience, and trust in God.[8]

Self-love is not a virtue, but rather a potential vice. Paul described himself as the chief of all the sinners (1 Timothy 1:15) and the least

---

7. Carin Rubenstein, "The Revolution Within," *Psychology Today*, August 1981, p. 81.
8. Paul C. Vitz, *Psychology as Religion: The Cult of Self-Worship* (Grand Rapids: Eerdmans, 1977), p. 91.

of all the saints (Ephesians 3:8). This is a spiritual reality and a holy humility that all need to realize. Leading a counselee down the primrose path of self-love is to return in ignorance to the Garden of Eden and to deny the purpose of the cross of Christ.

Love for God does not proceed from self-love, as many people who have been influenced by humanistic psychology seem to think and teach. Instead, love for God is the response to His love for us. John declares in his first epistle, "We love, because He first loved us" (4:19). Love for God and love for other people do not automatically follow love for self. Love for God and for neighbor comes from God Himself.

> The one who does not love does not know God, for God is love. By this the love of God was manifested in us, that God has sent His only begotten Son into the world so that we might live through Him. In this is love, not that we loved God, but that He loved us and sent His Son to be the propitiation for our sins. Beloved, if God so loved us, we also ought to love one another. (1 John 4:8-11)

The biblical order is this:

1. God loves individuals.
2. As they receive His love, they love Him, and as they love Him,
3. They love other people.

Unselfish, nonself-serving love comes from God. He is the source for the kind of love in which we all really need to be involved.

Secular humanism has effectively eroded the "great commandment" of God, and many in the church are responding to the call to "Love Yourself." Even Christians are preaching the message of self-love, erroneously thinking that if one loves himself he will then love others and God. In contradiction to the Bible, the new order is:

1. Love self, so that
2. You can love others
3. And God.

The Bible teaches that self-love is already there. When Jesus said to love your neighbor as yourself, he meant "as you already do." He did not even consider that people might not love themselves. "As thyself" is a given, not a third commandment. Even people who hate themselves do so as a result of self-love. People commit suicide from loving self enough to cut off the pain of living, or the frustration of responsibility, or the disappointment of not being good enough in terms of their own aspirations. Therefore, the answer cannot be self-love, but rather God's love and the person's love response to God. Love between persons (between God and human; between human and human) is the essential element to individual wholeness and social relationship.

The trend to "love yourself" reveals that we are truly living in the last days, for Paul wrote:

> But realize this, that in the last days difficult times will come. For men will be lovers of self, lovers of money, boastful, arrogant, revilers, disobedient to parents, ungrateful, unholy, unloving, irreconcilable, malicious gossips, without self-control, brutal, haters of good, treacherous, reckless, conceited, lovers of pleasure rather than lovers of God; holding to a form of godliness, although they have denied its power. (2 Timothy 3:1-5)

Paul is saying that self-love produces sin rather than love for God and love for people. If we follow the outcome of humanistic teachings of self-love we will see the elevation of personal pleasure over faithfulness to God. The answer for troubled people cannot be "love yourself."

Biblical counseling seeks to establish love where there has been a lack of love, and it seeks to redirect love that has been misdirected. The tendency of the natural man is to love self. But Scripture always encourages a person to love God more than anyone or anything else, and Scripture calls the person to love others as much as he already loves himself. To counsel Christians to love God and others at the expense of loving self is not a popular message today in the light of current admonishments to work toward self-worth and self-esteem. But the paradox of Scripture is that when we love God and others we actually have more love, joy, peace, and other fruits of the Spirit for ourselves.

THE BIBLICAL ALTERNATIVE TO SELF-LOVE

The alternative to self-love is not self-hatred, but rather a love relationship with God and loving relationships with people. The constant struggle that goes on between the flesh and the spirit is a struggle of love: self-love or other-directed love. Evidences of self-love are many. Here is a short list:

putting one's own comfort or well being over that of another,
believing self more than God, self-preoccupation,
giving undo attention to self's feelings or opinions,
self-condemnation (as self becomes its own god),
criticism of others,
blame,
not trusting God to do what is best for self,
desiring personal power,
competition,
self-defense,
thinking self is better than others,
becoming overly self-protective,
being overly affected by the opinion of others about self,
undo perfectionism.

Of course this list is limited, but it describes the focus of all of us as we tend to love self more than others. The attention is directed to self, and the motivation for action is for personal gain.

Numerous sins are related to some form of self-love. In fact, one could go through the Ten Commandments and see that these are directed at loving God through obedience to Him and at loving one's neighbor in specific ways. The sins that eat away at the soul, namely resentment and bitterness, originate in loving self more than loving God. Jealousy and envy also fit into this category. The sins of lust also come from self-directed love. Biblical counseling focuses on love as the means of change and redirects the counselee's love toward God and others.

The answer to our need for love is not to love ourselves more, but to love God and respond to His love. Love is meant to be directed outward, not inward. One way we most effectively love God is by loving each other, hence the inclusion of the second commandment with the first: love God; love neighbor. The apostle John echoes the Lord's commandment by saying:

No one has beheld God at any time; if we love one another, God abides in us, and His love is perfected in us.

And this commandment we have from Him, that the one who loves God should love his brother also. (1 John 4:12, 21)

We are to be givers and receivers of love. Those who need love need to receive it from God and people, and they need to love God and others as well.

13

Receiving and Giving Forgiveness

Forgiveness provides freedom from guilt, enables a person to walk in right relationship with God and man, and is the means for restoring a relationship that has been clouded by sin. Forgiveness is therefore one of the essential considerations in counseling. Both the receiving of forgiveness through confession and repentance and the giving of forgiveness to other individuals are important activities of counseling.

RECEIVING FORGIVENESS THROUGH CONFESSION AND REPENTANCE

God sent His Son to reverse the effects of sin. Jesus lived, died, and rose again to reestablish the love relationship between God and man. When a Christian sins he is acting as though he is not related to the Father in faith, hope, and love. But Jesus provided the way back to fellowship with God. Through confession, repentance, and forgiveness the believer can again respond to God in faith, hope, and love.

Since God forgives sin and restores believers as they confess and repent, one need not fear facing the reality of sin. A person no longer has to distort or deny actual points of failure. Within the context of God's mercy and truth, an individual may be receptive to seeing himself as he is: a person loved by God who needs forgiveness and transformation. Besides individual acts that fall short of God's standard, sin consists of attitudes of independence from God, unbelief, false hope or despair, and self-directed love. Sinful acts spring forth from those inner attitudes.

Forgiveness is available to all people on the basis of what Jesus did. To receive forgiveness requires recognition and admission of sin (confession), repentance (turning away from sin to go God's way), and believing that God is faithful to forgive and cleanse.

One biblical pattern for mental-emotional health and healing is a movement from sin to forgiveness through confession and repentance. The pattern was lived and practiced in both the Old and New Testaments. It has been a means of restoration and relief throughout the Christian church. As we take a panoramic view of the Bible, we see a system of sacrifices that began at Genesis and ended at the cross of Christ. These sacrifices were offered for Israel as a nation and for individual Israelites. In either case the pattern was the same. The sacrifices moved one from sin to forgiveness. The sacrifices were an admission of sin and an expression of repentance.

Psalm 32 is a beautiful example of the path from sin to forgiveness. Verses 3 and 4 and the beginning of verse 10 describe the condition of the individual living under the strain of unforgiven sin.

> When I kept silent about my sin, my body wasted away
> Through my groaning all day long.
> For day and night Thy hand was heavy upon me;
> My vitality was drained away as with the fever-heat of summer.
> Many are the sorrows of the wicked. . . .

Notice the mental and emotional anguish: "groaning all day long," "Thy hand was heavy upon me," and "Many are the sorrows." Also, notice the accompanying physical ailments: "my body wasted away" and "my vitality was drained away as with the fever-heat of summer." Mental-emotional strain affects the physical body when sin is known, but unconfessed. This does not mean that all sin results in physical illness or that all physical illness is the result of sin, but that the final condition of a person who lives under the weight of unforgiven sin may be mental-emotional and physical problems.

Because of the greatness of God's forgiveness, a person does not have to stay in sin and guilt. Verse 7 shows that God is a God of mercy because He is the one who delivers from sin:

Thou art my hiding place;
Thou dost preserve me from trouble;
Thou dost surround me with songs of deliverance.

God is indeed a place of refuge, a God who protects, and a God who delivers. In verse 5 the psalmist follows the pathway from sin to forgiveness:

I acknowledged my sin to Thee,
And my iniquity I did not hide;
I said, "I will confess my transgressions to the Lord";
And Thou didst forgive the guilt of my sin.

The person who repents and confesses is described in verses 1 and 2 as the one "whose transgression is forgiven, whose sin is covered!" David cries out: "How blessed is the man to whom the Lord does not impute iniquity, and in whose spirit there is no deceit!" His statement describes the forgiven person, as do verses 10 and 11:

But he who trusts in the Lord, lovingkindness shall surround him.
Be glad in the Lord and rejoice you righteous ones,
And shout for joy all you who are upright in heart.

After forgiveness, the person is called "righteous" and "upright in heart." He is fully cleansed from sin and has moved from the depths of despair to the heights of rejoicing.

After forgiveness, there is not only rejoicing, but also confidence because God will teach and guide:

I will instruct you and teach you in the way which you should go;
I will counsel you with My eye upon you.

(v. 8)

God wants to forgive, restore, and guide people away from sin. Before forgiveness, the mental and emotional burden is so heavy that it affects a person's entire body. After forgiveness, the burden lifts.

The pathway from sin to forgiveness through confession and repentance is a biblical route of relief for the troubled soul. It is the antidote the church has offered through the centuries to those suffering under sin. Biblical counseling offers God's remedy for sin and guilt through confession, repentance, and forgiveness.

Another scriptural example of the movement from sin to

forgiveness is the parable of the prodigal son from Luke 15. After the prodigal son spends his money in loose living and begins to starve, he recognizes his sin, repents of it, and confesses. He returns to his father and says, "I have sinned against heaven and in your sight; I am no longer worthy to be called your son" (vv. 18-19). Instead of condemnation or judgment, the father forgives and restores. Though the son deserves nothing, the father gives him the best robe for his back, a ring for his hand, and shoes for his feet. This is full forgiveness and full restoration.

The parable of the prodigal son illustrates how low a person may fall before he recognizes his sin, repents, and confesses. And the parable shows how eager and anxious God the Father is to have one person return to Him. While the sinner is yet far off in his journey back to God, our heavenly Father runs to him with open arms and administers His love and forgiveness. Such forgiveness is available to all who confess and repent.

When a person sins he puts himself under the law and into bondage. He tries to do better, but continues to fail until he receives the forgiveness of God through repentance and faith. Then he is able to receive the grace of God to serve righteousness. As he receives forgiveness and cleansing he is able to break out of this pattern and walk in the Spirit—at least until he falls again. But falling only comes when one slips back into the flesh and the law—self-effort. Again the way out is through confession, repentance, forgiveness, and walking again in the Spirit in the grace and power of God. Some Christians are sorry for their sins and confess and repent, but they fail to walk in the Spirit in full dependency on God.

Recognition of sin by conviction of the Holy Spirit is actually a positive process. If a person allows himself to be overwhelmed by condemnation, he prevents himself from correcting the error. If, however, he receives the correction with gratitude and faith and changes his course of thinking or acting, he will be able to walk in freedom. If the instruments on the panel of an airplane indicate that the pilot is going the wrong direction and the pilot responds by denying their validity or excusing his mistake or justifying himself or ignoring his error so that he will not feel guilty, he is headed for trouble. But if he notes the error (confesses) and makes the correction by turning around (repents), he will again be on the right course.

God is not keeping score on how many times a person sins. He is more interested in keeping His child on the right course. He has given His Word to indicate whether or not a believer is right on course. He has given the Holy Spirit to draw attention to the error and He has called fellow Christians to draw alongside. The biblical counselor comes alongside to act as an instrument to help a person choose to turn back onto God's course.

SELF-CONDEMNATION

When a person does not confess to God, repent, and believe God's forgiveness he falls prey to self-condemnation. Self-condemnation is a dangerous activity of pride, for it comes from self's playing the role of god. When self plays god he condemns, punishes, rewards, and excuses himself for behavior, depending upon whether he is a strict god (with high expectations—a perfectionist) or a lenient god (who tends to pamper and excuse self). When one condemns himself it is because he is disappointed that he did not perform as he or others think he should. God wants to be God in every area of life, especially in the area of judgment and mercy. He has the standard for behavior, and He grants pardon. Christians are called to live by His standard (not their own or the world's), and they are to be judged by Him. They can only judge themselves in His light and in agreement with Him, or they are in danger of misjudging. When they judge themselves in God's light, rather than receive condemnation from self and Satan, Christians may in humility receive forgiveness and cleansing from God.

Many Christians have been trapped in self-condemnation. It becomes a habit of thinking and responding to self as perhaps they have been thinking and responding to others—with criticism. Jesus warned, "Do not judge lest you be judged yourselves" (Matthew 7:1). Being critical of others is not only poor for relationships, but it also turns into self-condemnation. All condemnation is reserved for God, not for humans. We may discern right and wrong according to Scripture in order to modify our own behavior or turn another toward the Lord, but we may not condemn.

When a person chooses to act daily according to 1 John 1:9 and humble himself before God, admit the wrong to the Lord, and receive forgiveness and cleansing, he is free. When these things are taken care of immediately they do not pile up. Also, if one purposes to be merciful in thinking of others, then the guilt and self-condemnation that result from criticism will lose their power.

Pride often says, "I can't forgive myself." But, forgiving oneself is not the answer. Not once does Scripture tell us to forgive ourselves. When we forgive ourselves, we are trying to play God again, and there is no guarantee that we are indeed forgiven. In contrast, when God forgives us it is finished, signed, sealed, guaranteed, and forgotten. Receiving forgiveness from God and acting on His grace is an act of humility, faith, and gratitude. Not receiving and not believing God's forgiveness are acts of pride. Judas died in remorse and pride. Peter lived on the basis of the love and forgiveness of God. Peter changed from a prideful man to a man of humility when he believed and received the forgiveness of Jesus.

VERBAL CONFESSION

Because the only way back to God is through confession and receiving forgiveness, much biblical counseling will center on this essential activity. Forgiveness reestablishes the truth of the believer's relationship with God and cleanses the soul from guilt. Confession and forgiveness were among the primary activities in the cure-of-souls ministry. A person burdened down by guilt was able to confess sin, receive forgiveness, and repent or turn again to right thinking and acting. James stressed the importance of confessing sins to one another when he wrote, "Therefore, confess your sins to one another, and pray for one another, so that you may be healed. The effective prayer of a righteous man can accomplish much" (James 5:16).

From its early beginnings confession was made in the church. A great advantage of that practice is that there is something more definite and tangible about confessing to God in the presence of another because the sin and the forgiveness are right out in the open. Verbal confession to another person is especially helpful to people who fail to believe and receive God's forgiveness. A person in whom God lives can listen to a confession and then say, "Your sins are forgiven on the basis of 1 John 1:9."

> If we confess our sins, He is faithful to forgive us our sins and to cleanse us from all unrighteousness. (1 John 1:9)

Although he did not support compulsory confession, Martin Luther wrote:

I would let no man take confession away from me, and I would not give it up for all the treasures of the world, since I know what comfort and strength it has given me.[1]

Verbal confession strengthens the one who may doubt that he can be forgiven and gives him the opportunity to seal the confession and repentance with the prayer of another believer. Furthermore, there is an implied commitment to repentance. The one who has sinned is not alone in his struggle, but has a human advocate pleading his cause along with Jesus, his advocate with the Father.

Confession, forgiveness, repentance, and counsel go hand in hand. One purpose of counseling is to promote confession and repentance so that a person may be transformed into the image of Christ. James further wrote:

> My brethren, if any among you strays from the truth, and one turns him back, let him know that he who turns a sinner from the error of his way will save his soul from death, and will cover a multitude of sins. (James 5:19-20)

Such help does not come through criticism, but rather from loving availability to listen and to lead one into confession, forgiveness, and repentance. A counselor must be alert to listen for what might need to be confessed and then ask the counselee if he would like to confess to the Lord in his presence. Then after verbal confession, the counselor can assure the person of God's forgiveness on the basis of the cross and according to the promise of 1 John 1:9. He does not need to leave the counselee without helping him repent, however. Repentance is not just feeling sorry for sin, but returning to the love relationship with God and responding once again in faith, hope, and love. The counselor would explore with the counselee new ways of thinking and acting in response to his relationship with God.

A biblical counselor is quick to minister the forgiveness of God. This forgiveness is not just a whitewashing to cover up shortcomings, however. Forgiveness is a true washing away and only occurs when an individual honestly agrees with God in confession and repentance. Forgiveness, though freely given by God, is a costly act. Jesus

---

1. Martin Luther, Eighth Sermon of the series preached at Wittenberg after returning from Wartburg, 1522; in John T. McNeill, *A History of the Cure of Souls* (New York: Harper & Row, 1951), p. 168.

died to secure forgiveness for sin. Some people take the forgiveness of God lightly and do not move back into responding to His love in faith, responsibility, and submission. Others deny the forgiveness of God unless they *feel* forgiven. Forgiveness is a gift to be received in gratitude, in faith, and in renewed commitment to live in relationship with Him. When a person repents he responds to the love relationship with God through faith, hope, and love. Condemnation leads a person to continue in sin; forgiveness frees a person to walk in the Spirit.

Receiving God's forgiveness enhances the love relationship. When the Pharisee complained about the woman's washing Jesus' feet with her tears, Jesus taught that forgiveness enables a person to love more deeply. He said, "Her sins, which are many, have been forgiven, for she loved much; but he who is forgiven little, loves little" (Luke 7:47).

When one truly repents and receives forgiveness he is filled with both gratitude and love for the one who has expressed love. God's forgiveness springs from His great heart of love.

> The Lord is compassionate and gracious,
> Slow to anger and abounding in lovingkindness.
> He will not always strive with us;
> Nor will He keep His anger forever.
> He has not dealt with us according to our sins,
> Nor rewarded us according to our iniquities.
> For high as the heavens are above the earth,
> So great is His lovingkindness toward those who fear Him.
> As far as the east is from the west,
> So far has He removed our transgressions from us.
> (Psalm 103:8-12)

FORGIVING OTHERS

Because of the great forgiveness of God, the response of a Christian who has been forgiven is to forgive others. Jesus taught His followers to forgive one another, not just a few times but many multiples of times. Paul said, "Just as the Lord forgave you, so also should you" (Colossians 3:13). Just as sin separates people from God, sin separates people from people. Confession and forgiveness between persons, therefore, is the way of love. Forgiveness is an activity involved in loving neighbor as self and particularly in Christians loving one another as Jesus loves them.

When an individual truly understands the forgiveness of Jesus and what it cost Him to go to the cross, and when he has received this forgiveness from Jesus, then he will be able to forgive others. If he does not understand the significance of the cross, however, or if he does not think that he needs much forgiveness from God, then he may not be willing to forgive.

When we forgive someone, we ourselves bear the cost of the sin against us. Quite often the cost is high in terms of emotions, hurt feelings, and disappointment. Forgiveness, therefore, must be a choice more than a feeling. It is the choice and promise not to hold the sin against the offender any longer. It is an active response of love by one who is indwelt by God and who desires Jesus' life to be manifest through him. Forgiveness accepts the pain of the offense and foregoes the right to retaliation, bitterness, or resentment. If a person continues to hold something against another, forgiveness has not been accomplished.

Forgiveness begins in the inner person as he chooses to forgive even before the offender repents. An attitude of forgiveness enables the offended person to freely grant verbal forgiveness to the offender when he confesses and repents. An attitude of forgiveness prevents bitterness and resentment, but it does not prevent one from trying to make a situation right through confronting a fellow believer in love.

Unforgiveness takes its toll in poor relationships and even health problems. It keeps both the unforgiving and the unforgiven in bondage. Often roots of unforgiveness are buried deep and continue to keep the individual in patterns of thought and behavior that are destructive to himself and to others.

Unforgiveness often leaves an individual lonely and bitter. As the injustice or unforgiven sin forms a barrier to intimacy and compassion, sensitivity to the other person is replaced by protecting and justifying the self. Couples that complain they are having communication problems may be harboring unforgiveness. Resentment and bitterness are often difficult to deal with since they become absorbed into the character of the unforgiving one. But with God's help it is possible to overcome such patterns.

Besides creating barriers between people, unforgiveness alienates people from God. If an individual cannot experience the love and forgiveness of God, it may be that he is refusing to forgive another person. An unforgiving heart often stands between a person and the love of God. Bitterness hardens the heart from receiving God's love as well as the love of other people. If a person refuses to forgive, he is unable to receive what God has freely offered. Jesus was very clear in His warning concerning forgiveness.

> For if you forgive men for their transgressions, your heavenly Father will also forgive you. But if you do not forgive men, then your Father will not forgive your transgressions. (Matthew 6:14-15)

Many people live under condemnation and guilt because they have refused to forgive others.

The choice to forgive activates the work of the Holy Spirit in a person's life. When a person chooses to forgive, he acts according to the nature of God. He is doing exactly what the Lord is doing: forgiving. The choice to forgive releases the forgiver from further bitterness and resentment and frees him to keep on loving and living in relationship with God and other people. The choice to forgive also frees the offender to choose to do what is right.

Forgiveness also places trust in God to deal with both the offender and the results of the offense. Forgiveness releases both the forgiver and the forgiven one from a relationship of blame, retaliation, bitterness, and resentment. The choice to forgive releases the flow of God's love through the forgiving one.

As marvelous as the benefits of forgiveness are, believers do have to overcome certain hindrances to forgiveness. One common hindrance is to deny the offense or the hurt by failing to admit being wronged or by immediately moving into anger. Also, there is the human tendency to blame others in order to justify self. Often in the process of forgiveness one has to admit his own wrong in the situation. He may have to confess as well as forgive. However, the confession may not include accusation such as: "Please forgive me for getting angry at you for your thoughtlessness."

Some people fear that if they forgive they are simply freeing the offender to repeat the offense. Forgiveness is not passive; it is actually the choice that frees us to change the situation or solve the problem that may have led to the offense. Finally, failure to forgive may result from focusing on the personal hurt and dwelling on the injustice rather than choosing to love the other person as much as self.

The counselor needs to explain the principles and source of forgiveness so that the person may forgive not only occasional offenses, but subsequent repetitions of offense (Luke 17:3-4). Since humanity cannot fully experience the flow of forgiveness in the face of injustice, violence, rejection, anger, and hurt, there is a desperate need for divine forgiveness to flow through the offended believer. Just as Jesus forgave each person, He is living within the believer to forgive. Forgiveness is a joint act. Jesus enables believers to forgive as they choose to forgive. On the other hand, unwillingness to forgive is sin and separates the unforgiving one from God.

The world is not a just place, but there is a just God who also loves and forgives. Much anguish comes from injustice. If a person attributes the injustice to God, then he will not understand the love and forgiveness of God. Therefore, a counselor may need to spend a great deal of time teaching about the character of God, the justice of God, and the forgiveness of God so that the counselee will be willing to forgive and be forgiven.

When one truly chooses to forgive, the act is accomplished by the will and enabled by the Holy Spirit. However, the counselor might outline for the counselee these steps to forgiving:

1. Tell God about the situation, confess your sins, and ask Him to bring healing, forgiveness, and the ability to forgive.
2. Consider the greatness of the forgiveness of God and the great cost of the cross of Christ.
3. Choose to forgive and not to hold the offense against the offender.
4. If you yourself have sinned against the offender, go to him and confess your own sin and ask forgiveness without casting blame or even expecting him to ask forgiveness of you.
5. Maintain the attitude of forgiveness and resist the temptation to nurse past wounds.
6. If unforgiveness or bitterness recur because of reminders or because the sin is repeated, maintain the choice to forgive in the will even if the feelings are slow to catch up.

If a counselee continues to be hurt about the offense or to have feelings of unforgiveness after having chosen to forgive, the counselor may ask the following questions:

1. Are you still hurt? If so, remember that some personal wounds may not heal as rapidly as the choice to forgive.

Feelings of being hurt are not always an indication of unforgiveness.

2. Do you choose by your actions not to require payment for the offense in terms of retaliation or the desire for the offender to suffer for his acts?

3. Do you pray that God will forgive and bless the offender?

After asking these questions, the counselor may advise the counselee not to dwell on the offense and not to bring it up in conversation with others. In choosing to forget by purposefully not thinking or speaking about the offense, the counselee will indeed forget, and the hurt feelings will disappear.

As well as teaching counselees to forgive, counselors need to help them to confess and ask forgiveness of others as well. Quite often when someone has been offended, he himself has offended the other person. Admitting wrong and asking forgiveness may be far more humiliating than extending forgiveness. However, in many cases confession of wrong opens the way for the other person to confess so that mutual forgiveness and healing may occur. In asking forgiveness, it is wise to verbally admit having wronged the person and then specifically ask, "Will you forgive me?" Just saying, "I'm sorry," is not enough because it does not include the confession or the request.

In dealing with bitterness and resentment that have developed from unforgiveness of offenses from the past, the choice to forgive in the present will bring release and healing. However, many people attempt to relieve themselves of wrong feelings by going into the past and trying to remember past offenses. Rather than delving into the past and reviewing, rehearsing, and renursing past wounds, it is more helpful to choose to forgive in the present. If a counselee happens to recall a past offense he can choose to forgive the offender. But if he does not recall past offenses he does not have to be concerned, because choices to forgive present offenses will serve to release a person from the bondage of bitterness and resentment that may have become internalized. As a person develops the new response of forgiveness based upon the vast forgiveness of Christ, the new choices will replace the former patterns.

Each time something negative touches a person he can indulge himself in a bit of hurt feelings or he can choose to forgive. Often a person does not even think to forgive because the offending person has no idea that he has done anything wrong. But whenever there is even the slightest of hurts, it is cleansing and freeing to forgive. Otherwise each hurt accumulates until there is a great pile of wounds that just one additional offense can topple. It's like moment-by-moment picking up after oneself or letting the house become more and more cluttered until there is absolute chaos.

Internalized or expressed angry thoughts can turn into an attitude of wrath and result in guilt over the bitter thoughts or angry explosions. Such a pattern of internalized or expressed anger can be changed by the choice to forgive.

> Let all bitterness and wrath and anger and clamor and slander be put away from you, along with all malice. And be kind to one another, tender-hearted, forgiving each other, just as God in Christ also has forgiven you. (Ephesians 4:31-32)

A biblical counselor needs to be sensitive to the accumulation of hurt and the possible patterns of self-defense by which a person may respond. He needs to gently, but faithfully, bring the person to a new pattern of response.

As a person chooses to forgive, he will find that the sooner he forgives, the less damage is done. If a person waits three hours before forgiving an offender in his heart, he allows three hours for the seeds of bitterness and resentment to take hold, and he wastes three hours of emotional energy on anger and self-pity that he could be using in a positive way. The time may be three minutes or even three seconds, or one may fall into bondage for years. The choice is up to the injured party.

It may be costly to forgive because one thereby forsakes the so-called right of revenge. Yet forgiveness is worth the cost because the love of God brings healing and renewed relationships. As one chooses to forgive he is released to identify with the very character of God. He comes to understand God's continual and sacrificial act of forgiveness. He begins to identify with God in God's constant activity—forgiving. As he forgives others as God forgives him, he finds God working in him and he is strengthened. By choosing to forgive and by receiving from the Lord the ability to forgive, he is thus able to move out of the bondage of unforgiveness, bitterness, resentment, and depression.

Because Jesus paid the price for sin on the cross, He made

forgiveness available to all people. After confession, forgiveness cleanses an individual from guilt, frees him to pursue righteous thinking and acting, opens the channel of love, and fully restores relationship. Whenever there is hurt, breakdown in communication, self-justification, blame, or anger, a biblical counselor needs to help the counselee receive and give forgiveness.

14

Inner and Outer Change

Biblical counseling deals with both the inner man and the outer man—with thoughts and emotions and with words and actions. For a Christian to live a consistent life, his thoughts, emotions, words, and actions must cooperate with the indwelling Holy Spirit. Therefore, a spiritual counselor will desire to help an individual with both the inner and the outer life.

Much of the Old Testament law dealt with a code of external behavior. But even the Ten Commandments include both the inner and outer man. For instance, when God said that man is to worship Him only (inner action), He also said that there were to be no idols before Him (outer action). The psalms are full of inner thoughts, feelings, and choices that lead to external actions.

> Thy word I have treasured in my heart,
> That I may not sin against Thee.
> (Psalms 119:11)

Note the combination of attitude and activity, knowledge and understanding, and singing and speaking in Psalm 100.

> Shout joyfully to the Lord, all the earth.
> Serve the Lord with gladness;
> Come before Him with joyful singing.
> Know that the Lord Himself is God;

It is He who has made us, and not we ourselves;
We are His people and the sheep of His pasture.

Enter His gates with thanksgiving,
And His courts with praise.
Give thanks to Him; bless His name.
For the Lord is good;
His lovingkindness is everlasting,
And His faithfulness to all generations.

Jesus further emphasized the relationship of inner thoughts, understanding, and desire with outer actions and words.

For the mouth speaks out of that which fills the heart. The good man out of his good treasure brings forth what is good; and the evil man out of his evil treasure brings forth what is evil. (Matthew 12:34-35)

Particularly in the Sermon on the Mount, Jesus identified sinful inner attitudes that were beneath external deeds.

In the psychological world there is argument between those counselors who deal with behavior and those who deal with thought. As far as the Bible is concerned both are important. Proverbs 16:3 says, "Commit thy works unto the Lord, and thy thoughts shall be established" (KJV). A person needs to be encouraged to choose right thoughts and right actions. In Romans 10 we see the combination of belief (thinking) and action (confession):

That if you confess with your mouth Jesus as Lord, and believe in your heart that God raised Him from the dead, you shall be saved; for with the heart man believes, resulting in righteousness, and with the mouth he confesses, resulting in salvation. (Romans 10:9-10)

Here is an internal choice of belief combined with an external action of confession. The requirement of both thought and action is seen also in James where he says, "Faith without works is dead." Faith, an internal choice, is dead without works, external action. Choosing to think and to act will involve and affect the whole being.

What a person does influences his thoughts, and what a person thinks influences what he does. Sinful thoughts can eventually lead to sinful behavior. The person who gets involved in adultery has been thinking adulterous thoughts. Conversely, thoughts often conform to behavior. People may even distort Scripture to fit their behavior. For example, those in homosexual churches believe that the Bible condones homosexuality.

The lust of the flesh, the lust of the eyes, and the pride of life (1 John 2:16) appeal to the outer man. Satan attempts to confuse or tempt people into believing that the things that appeal to lust and pride are not only realities of life, but necessities as well. The one who believes this lie misses the true reality that exists in the inner man.

The external law may only touch the outer man and be unable to reach the inner man. On the other hand, the law of the Spirit, which is the law of love, gives life to the inner man so that he can be transformed from the inside out. Every problem of living has its spiritual counterpart. Treating the results of lust and pride apart from the inner man will only strengthen the outer man. But touching the spirit of a person with God's love will transform every facet of his being.

In spiritual counseling there are intertwined inner and outer works. The inner work has to do with faith in God, a renewed desire to love God and others, and being renewed in the spirit of the mind. It combines the work of the Holy Spirit with the person's response of faith, hope, and love—it involves thinking and feeling. The outer renewal consists of new ways of behaving that are consistent with biblical principles.

CHANGES IN THINKING

Change occurs on the inside and outside as a Christian chooses to give himself to God to be transformed by the renewing of the mind, for the resultant behavior shows "what the will of God is, that which is good and acceptable and perfect" (Romans 12:2).

Jesus promised that He would set people free from bondage by revealing truth. "If you abide in My word, then you are truly disciples of Mine; and you shall know the truth, and the truth shall make you free" (John 8:31-32). As a person thinks according to the truth God has given in the Bible, he finds freedom to bring his emotions and his actions into line with God's truth. Abiding in God's Word means more than casual believing; abiding implies thinking, feeling, and acting according to faith in God's Word. Jesus said that as people abide in His Word they are His learners. He continues to teach them the truth that sets them free. Wrong thinking causes havoc in emotions and error in actions, but when a person's thoughts, feelings, and actions are based on the Bible, he receives wisdom, peace, righteousness, and the excellent fruit of the Spirit.

Paul wrote, "The righteous man shall live by faith." (Galatians 3:11) The power of faith in a person's life will direct his thinking, feeling, and acting. Unfortunately some of the most influential forms of faith that compel twentieth-century thinking, feeling, and acting are based upon secular humanistic psychological opinion rather than upon biblical truth.

GOD'S TRUTH AND ACCURATE THINKING

Erroneous thinking often gets a person into deep misery and complicated conflicts. Therefore, one of the primary concerns in biblical counseling is truth itself. Besides bringing out the truth of God, a biblical counselor will watch for error or distortion in a counselee's thinking and speaking. He will attempt to help the person to recognize wrong thinking and to consider how Jesus might think in such a situation.

One debilitating form of wrong thinking is concentrating only on the problem. The individual becomes so problem-oriented that even a nearby solution may not be seen. Paul speaks of thinking in Philippians:

> Finally, brethren, whatever is true, whatever is honorable, whatever is right, whatever is pure, whatever is lovely, whatever is of good repute, if there is any excellence and if anything worthy of praise, let your mind dwell on these things. (Philippians 4:8)

Paul is speaking of more than just positive thinking. He is encouraging believers to focus their attention on what is right or what can be right and true in a situation. Rather than stewing about what cannot be done, it is often helpful to consider what can be done, even though it may be very small. The problem itself may look too large to tackle all at once, but maybe one small change can be made in the right direction. For instance, a parent may not be able to do anything directly about a grown child's marriage problems, but the parent can continue to love, pray, and perhaps encourage without condemnation, pressure, or interference. If, on the other hand, that parent worries and stews over the situation, he may make matters worse and waste considerable emotional energy.

The old question about whether the glass is half-full or half-empty sometimes reveals an individual's view of life. Paul emphasizes thinking about that which is full, but many people see life as a half empty glass. They see what is missing instead of what is provided. A counselee with this kind of thinking needs to be brought into a closer relationship with God by receiving God's love and by thanking God for what He has given him. As the love of God is received and as thoughts center more on Jesus, the thought life changes. As the counselee through conversation is convinced of the love of God, he will see the half of the glass that is filled and experience gratitude.

A grateful heart brings joy and contentment to a person. Gratitude and praise come from focusing on who God is and what He has provided, not on circumstances. It is not always enough, however, to tell someone he should be grateful. In some instances the person then adds the lack of gratitude to his half-empty glass. In encouraging gratitude the counselor needs to tactfully help focus the thinking without being critical. A counselor should not ignore the half-empty glass or pretend that it does not exist. He may need to spend some time identifying with the counselee by looking at the half-empty glass—but then he should draw the counselee along to focus on the part that is full.

It is a blessing in counseling to see the person with a half-empty glass move to seeing the glass half-filled and then to see it filled to "good measure, pressed down, shaken together, running over" (Luke 6:38).

Individuals with distorted thinking who experience problems of living become transformed by the love of God. As their thought life changes, their behavior changes also. There are countless testimonies to this transforming power of God's love from the day of Pentecost to the present. And until the Lord returns again it is the most powerful force for meeting life's problems.

Accurate thinking will free a counselee from the bondage of internal deception and gross generalities. Deception originated from Satan himself, that father of lies. Any time he can cloud an issue or alter the truth, he can gain a foothold in the mind. This is what he did with Eve. Many people carry lies around in their minds as facts. Most of this internal lying centers in self and comes from having accepted and believed false assumptions about self and about God. Many of these lies are in the form of generalizations, which may need to be probed in the counseling session. Quite often even negative generalities are protective devices which prevent one from dealing with real problems.

Since the Bible is the spiritual counselor's book of truth, all that is said in a counseling conversation may be evaluated in terms of the Bible. For instance, a revealing statement such as "God is not as good to me as He is to everybody else" may be examined under God's light. It may not appear that God is as good to one as to another, but His goodness is extended to all persons, whether good or bad (Matthew 5:45). Such erroneous thinking comes from not knowing God and thus provides a key for the counselor: the need to spend time teaching about the character of God. When a counselee says, "Everybody treats me unfairly," unfair treatment can be explored in terms of Jesus' experience. In fact, one can be led into a deeper understanding of Christ's character through experiencing sufferings similar to those He endured. The counselor will not just counter erroneous thinking with the truth, but will help the counselee explore reality by asking questions and offering alternatives in the perspective of the Bible. There are numerous opportunities to bring honesty and reality into a counseling conversation, not for the sake of argument, but for new understanding. Therefore, the counselor will want to keep the truth of God ever before him so that he can listen carefully and help the counselee examine his own thoughts and beliefs to see if they are true.

Imaginations and falsehoods form strongholds in the mind and will. The mind is a battleground on which thoughts from the world, the flesh, and the devil vie against the truth of God. Human beings can easily be deceived. Therefore, they need to be following the Spirit in order to combat falsehoods. Together the counselee and counselor may look at thoughts and ideas within the context of God's mercy and truth. Paul declares:

> For though we walk in the flesh, we do not war after the flesh: (For the weapons of our warfare are not carnal, but mighty through God to the pulling down of strong holds;) Casting down imaginations, and every high thing that exalteth itself against the knowledge of God, and bringing into captivity every thought to the obedience of Christ. (2 Corinthians 10:3-5, KJV)

Imaginations include fears, doubts, and other thoughts not substantiated by the Bible. Erroneous thinking undermines a person's walk with the Lord and takes precedence over the knowledge of God. Therefore, both the counselor and the counselee need to bring "into captivity every thought to the obedience of Christ" and to weigh every idea with the truth of Scripture. When thinking is confused or certain thoughts seem to take hold of the mind, a counselee needs to hear, read, and think about the Word of God. Just reading several chapters of the Bible often brings a sense of peace and stability.

CHANGES IN EMOTIONS

In biblical counseling, the counselor encourages the counselee to believe what God has said over and above his own feelings. Because feelings are deep and because they are close to the very heart of man, they appear difficult to change. But the Lord can change them by renewing the mind of the counselee (Romans 12:1-2 and Ephesians 4:23). The counselee's thought life has previously been formed by his natural environment, which has been influenced by Satan. Circumstances and past experiences have played a large part in the development of patterns of feeling, and in many instances feelings govern a person. Because of hurts and distortions of perception, feelings are often unreliable indicators of truth. Thus, certain feelings may tell one just the opposite of what is true.

Emotions may range from the sublime to the sinful. When feelings and desires agree with the indwelling Holy Spirit they are good, beautiful, and even holy. But when they originate in the flesh, they become focused on self and grieve the Holy Spirit. The counselor will want to be sure that the counselee does not deny the existence of feelings and desires. But he will want to assist the person to bring those feelings and desires to the Lord. Just as a person can change his thinking by putting on Christ and by believing God's Word, so also a counselee can change his emotions by putting on Christ and believing God's Word.

When a counselee chooses to trust and obey God more than his own feelings and when he believes God's Word more than his own limited experience, he allows God to perform His work of renewing the mind. The emotions may scream and shout even after a person puts them under submission to the truth of God's Word, but eventually such feelings will be transformed. As an individual is faithful to obey God, he may confidently ask God to give him the emotions that match the obedience. As thoughts are released from bondage of distortion and the person chooses to obey God, the emotions will gradually conform to the Word of God as well.

In biblical counseling the greatest single force for changing the emotions is the love of God revealed in His Word and through His Holy Spirit. Although many emotions will surface in counseling, we will discuss just a few of the major emotions that can become detrimental in a person's life. "Perfect love casts out fear," heals personal hurts, replaces wrong anger, and changes rejection to acceptance. All emotions can be transformed through God's love as it is believed, received, and given in return.

FEAR

One feeling everyone experiences at different times is fear. Some fear, such as the fear of fire, is healthy and prevents one from foolish actions. But fear often manifests itself in debilitating ways and prevents rational responses to life's situations and problems. God's Word says, "For God hath not given us the spirit of fear; but of power, and of love, and of a sound mind" (2 Timothy 1:7, KJV). When fear is an accurate response to present danger it is good and natural, but when fear is connected to the past or future in such a way as to be out of proportion to the present situation and to prevent one from acting responsibly, that fear is to be regarded as coming from the flesh. One can overcome fleshly fear by drawing close to God and remembering His caring nature and His power to keep us. The psalmist recognized the difference between his own feelings and the truth of God when he declared:

> My flesh and my heart may fail;
> But God is the strength of my heart
> and my portion forever.
> (Psalm 73:26)

David wrote:

> The Lord is my light and my salvation;
> Whom shall I fear?
> The Lord is the defense of my life;
> Whom shall I dread?
> (Psalms 27:1)

A person may read many other Scriptures to overcome feelings of fear. As these living words from the Bible are given precedence over fleshly thoughts and feelings, fear can be conquered. As one exercises faith by choice over feelings, he will appropriate the victory that Christ has already won.

As a person develops faith in God rather than merely in his environment and in old ways of doing things, he more easily overcomes fear. As trust is nurtured and maintained, the spiritual response becomes a person's normal response. As he begins to walk by faith in more and more areas of his life, he learns by experience that God is there to guide, direct, enable, forgive, heal, and restore. No longer does a person have to rely solely on himself and other people. The person will find it easier to choose to submit to God's rulership and meet problems God's way.

ANGER AND HURT

Hurt and anger often need to be dealt with in counseling. These are basic responses to situations in which an individual believes that serious wrong has occurred to him or to others in his environment. But these emotions may become more than responses when they are allowed to rule. Emotions are related to thinking. For instance, responses of hurt and anger are far greater if we suspect that someone hurt us on purpose rather than by accident. How we think about a person or situation will greatly determine the response and the intensity of the response.

Anger and hurt are closely related. Some people move immediately into anger without even realizing the hurt, whereas others remain in hurt and self-pity. Both responses can become strongholds in the emotions if they are given free reign and are supported with excuses and reasons for being hurt or angry. Expressing such emotions and even talking about them may increase them unless the thinking moves from the point of injury to forgiveness and possible solutions.

Knowing and acting according to the truth of God enables individuals to overcome explosive expressions and internally prolonged anger which may lead to wrath, bitterness, and depression. Changed thinking is a great help for those who have problems with anger. For a period of time, ventilation therapies were quite popular. In such forms of psychotherapy, people were encouraged to express their anger both verbally and physically. In some instances, props such as dummy bags were used so that a person could imagine the enemy and strike the dummy.

Although many psychotherapists have encouraged the expression of anger as a remedy, research shows that ventilation of anger does not make it go away, but rather increases it.[1] On the other hand, looking at the situation from the other person's point of view seems to curtail anger. In other words, thinking influences emotions. Emotions are not independent. They have to be nursed and expressed and encouraged to remain by thinking the kinds of thoughts that will prolong them.

Initial hurt or anger may be an internal reaction, but when it is expressed in retaliatory actions, sin may be involved. In investigating both anger and hurt, the counselor needs to help the counselee see the line between the feeling and the external response. The Bible says, "Be angry, and yet do not sin; do not let the sun go down on your anger. . . . Let all bitterness and wrath and anger and clamor and slander be put away from you, along with all malice" (Ephesians 4:26, 31).

Confidence in God as sovereign and just strengthens a person so that he does not have to react in anger. Proverbs 14:29 gives wisdom concerning anger: "He who is slow to anger has great understanding, but he who is quick-tempered exalts folly." Even when things are wrong, Psalms 37:8 urges: "Cease from anger, and forsake wrath; fret not yourself, it leads only to evildoing."

Jesus expressed anger against the evil practices of those using the House of God as a marketplace (John 2:13-17). His anger stimulated Him into righteous action, even though the moneychangers would not agree. Anger over wrongdoing, if channeled into godly action, can be a stimulus for good. But this is a rare use of anger, since most anger does not result in godly action.

Some people have developed such a habit of flying off the handle that it takes some time to develop new ways of acting. They continue a pattern of anger that worked for them as children. While they were growing up they got their way through temper tantrums or other emotional displays, such as pouting, and they just continue the basic pattern in a more "adult" fashion. A counselee can learn to see that an initial angry response may be used as a signal to quickly turn

---

1. Carol Tavris, *Anger: The Misunderstood Emotion* (New York: Simon and Schuster, 1982).

to God for guidance. Looking at a situation from God's perspective may lead people who have formerly been destructive in their anger to turn their energy to solving problems God's way. Each incident of anger may provide another opportunity to choose a new way of acting so that problem solving with the wisdom and strength of God will replace the expression of wrath.

Chronic anger may be due to bitterness about circumstances, resentment against God, and unforgiveness of people. Chronic anger may stem from wanting one's own way and not getting it. A habitual attitude of anger affects every thought, emotion, and action. Only choosing to believe the goodness of God, choosing to relinquish one's will to Him, and choosing to forgive others will bring the needed change.

REJECTION

A feeling of rejection often includes loneliness, self-pity, depression, rebellion, and even suicide. Everyone experiences rejection at some time in life to some degree. But people who have suffered much rejection throughout life are tempted to develop a response pattern that leads to even more feelings of rejection. In fact, quite often they feel rejected when they are not being rejected at all.

An individual with a rejection pattern may try to gain acceptance and approval through performance, may retreat from others to prevent further rejection, or may become indifferent and hard. The outward signs may not be at all identical. Some people who have suffered much rejection may escape into fantasy or imagination. Some may dwell in self-pity and envy others. Some may set themselves apart as judges of others. Some may be overly sensitive to what other people say or do and will interpret correction as rejection. Rejection may lead to external rebellion and hatred, or it may lead to bitterness and self-pity.

God's remedy for rejection is His great love. Only divine love can heal the deep wounds of rejection. The woman at the well had been rejected in several marriages and was an outcast of her city, but she was restored by God's love. Joseph was rejected by his brothers, but he was kept in God's love. David was rejected by King Saul and by his wife Michal, but he was sustained by God's love. Moses was often rejected by the people of Israel, but he knew God. When a person knows the love of God, rejection from people does not have as devastating an effect.

It is especially important for Christians to learn how to deal with rejection since the Bible teaches that believers will be rejected. The most complete picture of rejection in the Bible is that of the Lord Jesus. From His unique conception until His death on the cross, Jesus suffered rejection. As one traces His life, one can see angry rejection by the scribes and Pharisees, misunderstanding from even His own family, the quiet rejection of disappointed crowds unwilling to hear the message He had to give them, deceitful rejection by Judas, abandonment by His disciples, and denial by Peter. Then on the cross He suffered the rejection of ridicule and scorn as well as pain. No one has been rejected as much as Jesus.

Since He is our model, a biblical counselor will want to teach about the rejection of Jesus, the reason for that rejection, and Jesus' response. Jesus suffered all to secure our salvation because of God's great love for every person. His response to rejection could only then be love. He was rejected for love and responded in love; he was rejected so that mankind could be forgiven, and he responded by praying, "Father, forgive them; for they do not know what they are doing" (Luke 23:34).

Jesus was able to respond with forgiveness because He knew the love of the Father, even though He did not feel the love of God during the dark hours on the cross. A Christian likewise may respond with forgiveness on the same basis: knowing the love of the Father, even when he does not *feel* that love with his emotions. The love of the Father for Jesus is extended to the believer. When Jesus prayed on the night of His betrayal, He said:

> I do not ask in behalf of these alone, but for those also who believe in Me through their word; that they may all be one; even as Thou, Father, art in Me, and I in Thee, that they also may be in Us; that the world may believe that Thou didst send Me. And the glory which Thou hast given Me I have given to them; that they may be one, just as We are one; I in them, and Thou in Me, that they may be perfected in unity, that the world may know that Thou didst send Me, and didst love them, even as Thou didst love Me. (John 17:20-23, KJV)

The very same love that enabled Jesus to forgive is given to the believer as he faces rejection.

The answer to rejection is more of Jesus—more of His love, life, and truth in the believer—and less of self (wounded and rejected). When a Christian is rejected he may respond with the works of the flesh or the fruit of the Spirit. When he knows the love of God and chooses to walk in His Spirit, the response will be the fruit of the Spirit. All trials, including rejection, test the fruit of the tree. Relationship with Jesus replaces rejection so that love replaces loneliness, and forgiveness replaces the pattern of negative responses.

CHANGES IN BEHAVIOR

As God transforms the thinking and the emotions, the external behavior changes as well. When one is renewed in his mind and lives by God's love, His actions will conform to the Word of God. But there are times when changing behavior will affect the emotions and the thinking. C. S. Lewis wisely wrote:

> Do not waste time bothering whether you "love" your neighbour; act as if you did. As soon as we do this we find one of the great secrets. When you are behaving as if you loved someone, you will presently come to love him.[2]

Choosing actions that agree with the Word of God will cause a person to be transformed in thoughts and emotions as well, as long as the motivation is to obey God rather than to manipulate one's own will. For instance, if a person thinks gossiping thoughts and feels like gossiping, but holds his tongue out of obedient love for the Lord, he will gain victory in both the emotions and the thinking.

Although we are not saved by good behavior, choosing to speak and act according to God's Word should be the result of being a Christian. God saved us by grace, not because of our works, but good works follow: "For we are His workmanship, created in Christ Jesus for good works, which God prepared beforehand, that we should walk in them" (Ephesians 2:10). The Bible is filled with directions for behavior in both speaking and acting. Ruling the tongue is emphasized in Proverbs, Ephesians, and James. Conducting oneself in consideration for others and in obedience to God is discussed throughout the Bible. Therefore, rather than just listing specific behavior, we would encourage the counselor and counselee to go directly to the Word for instructions on behavior.

Principles for biblical behavior are generally better known than

2. C. S. Lewis, *Mere Christianity* (1943; reprint ed., New York: MacMillan, 1960), p. 116.

obeyed. God's love will enable a person to obey what he knows to be true, and God's truth will reveal the kind of behavior that is consistent with the indwelling Holy Spirit. In counseling, the emphasis is on the love relationship with God that enables a person to do His will, but at the same time obedience may be approached through thinking according to God's Word, feeling the emotions that come from God's love, and doing what is right even if the thinking and feeling do not fully agree. Then as the counselee learns to live as God has called him to live, he will find that his thoughts, emotions, and actions all coordinate together with the Word of God and the indwelling Holy Spirit.

After teaching God's principles for living in the Sermon on the Mount, Jesus said:

> Therefore every one who hears these words of Mine, and acts upon them, may be compared to a wise man, who built his house upon the rock. And the rain descended, and the floods came, and the winds blew, and burst against that house; and yet it did not fall, for it had been founded upon the rock. (Matthew 7:24-25)

Biblical counseling attempts to help people build their lives on the solid rock of God's truth.

CHOICE FOR CHANGE

Christianity cannot be divorced from thinking, feeling, and behaving, and change is a process that continues throughout a Christian's walk. It is a walk of choice and change, from old to new, from sin to sanctification, from error to truth, from death to life, from self to Him. Such change is a primary function of the Body of Christ until each person is transformed into His likeness.

Individuals do have a measure of choice which carries with it a comparable degree of responsibility. Choices are made to think, feel, and act in certain ways. Referring persons to the psychological way is sending them to a competing system of thinking, feeling, and acting. There is no better system of thought, emotion, and behavior than that revealed in Scripture. Biblical choices elevate the spirit over the flesh and establish new habits for old ones. New habits built upon biblical principles will then establish the believer in his walk with the Lord.

15

Activities for Change

Just listening and talking and discovering God's ways once a week in the conversation of counseling may not be enough. Talking and hearing about the way of change and not doing anything about it can be a waste of time. James warns,

> But prove yourselves doers of the word, and not merely hearers who delude themselves. For if any one is a hearer of the word and not a doer, he is like a man who looks at his natural face in a mirror; for once he has looked at himself and gone away, he has immediately forgotten what kind of person he was. But one who looks intently at the perfect law, the law of liberty, and abides by it, not having become a forgetful hearer but an effectual doer, this man shall be blessed in what he does. (James 1:22-25)

Change requires doing something different. Therefore, during most counseling sessions the counselee and counselor need to agree on some actual, tangible activities to do during the week. The purpose of the activities is to bring an individual closer to God.

These activities may include reading and meditating on a specific section of God's Word and finding ways to apply the Scripture in actual living; praying in agreement with Scripture; and/or doing something very practical, such as forgiving someone or developing a new habit. The counselee is not the only person with work to do; the counselor also needs to be reading and applying the same sections of Scripture in his own life and praying for the counselee. Thus, in bringing about change there is an agreement made by both partners.

INVOLVEMENT IN THE BODY OF CHRIST

We strongly encourage church participation as part of the counselees' regular weekly activities. Nearly always, when a couple or individual comes in for counseling, we encourage involvement in corporate worship, small-group fellowship, and person-to-person relationships for greater opportunity for growth, change, and victory over problems of living. Whether churches are large or small, the usual Sunday morning service needs to be supplemented by a small-group relationship of some kind. Sometimes small Sunday school classes can provide the personal involvement necessary for Christian growth. But usually a small home group provides a more intimate, supportive environment for change. In addition to the small home group, we recommend that individuals and couples find at least one other individual or couple in the fellowship with whom they can share.

This immersion in all three levels of church life is of great value. We have rejoiced to see how the Lord has gathered just the right persons around those who are suffering. In this way, the ministry is shared in such a manner as to give full credit to God. One plants, another waters, but God brings about the growth. "For we are God's fellow-workers; you are God's field, God's building" (1 Corinthians 3:9). Although the individual or couple experiencing problems will in most cases not share deep problems with a small group or on an individual or couple-to-couple basis, these times will provide an opportunity for love to flow between persons so that change and support will occur. All of the love given and received on these three levels of relationship is to encourage that closer walk with God which each Christian needs to have.

The change that occurs is due to love. The continual expression of love given to the counselee and received and expressed by the counselee will transform the life. The counselor and others provide the environment for change (love); the conversations the counselor and counselee have provide the direction for change (biblical principles); the receiving and responding is up to the counselee.

READING AND MEDITATING ON GOD'S WORD

Daily involvement in the Word is essential. A counselor may suggest passages of Scripture to be studied in a number of ways: through certain prepared Bible studies, through questions that arise during the counseling conversation, through an assignment of verses that emphasize one or more aspects of God's character, through suggestions of ways to meditate on God's Word, through encouragement to memorize Scripture, and through tying the Word of God with a specific application to be performed. The Scriptures learned should be mainly those that set forth the mercy and truth of God, and the applications performed should be tied to Scriptures of love expressed.

Listening to tapes of Scripture is especially helpful to those who learn best through auditory means. Some people benefit greatly by hearing their own voices reading Scripture aloud or on tape. Also, consistent church attendance gives one the opportunity to feed further on the Word and to hear practical applications.

God changes people from the inside out, but one can cooperate with God by putting Scripture into his mind and heart. The Word of God is true and living. It brings power from the invisible world into a person's life. As a counselee and counselor receive the Word of God, they are nourishing themselves with supernatural strength and supernatural wisdom. There is also a supernatural working of the Word which heals persons, discerns the deep thoughts and motivations of individuals, and transforms believers into the image of Christ as they respond and obey. No wonder the psalmist loved the Word!

> I will meditate on Thy precepts,
> And regard Thy ways.
>
> I shall delight in Thy statues;
> I shall not forget Thy word. . . .
>
> How sweet are Thy words to my taste!
> Yes, sweeter than honey to my mouth!
>
> From Thy precepts I get understanding:
> Therefore I hate every false way.

Thy word is a lamp to my feet,
And a light to my path.
(Psalm 119:15, 16, 103-5)

Counselor and counselee alike need not only to read the Word,
but also to chew it and digest it. Meditating on the Word and
memorizing those verses that particularly apply to the needs of the
counselee give the Holy Spirit the opportunity to indicate practical,
personal applications. For instance, meditating on John 15 and
seeking applications for abiding in Christ can be very fruitful. In fact,
understanding these verses comes primarily through practicing
abiding in Christ. What does abiding in Christ mean when the
children are fussing or sick? What does abiding mean when plans are
spoiled? What does abiding mean when someone has just hurt you
with a wounding remark? When does abiding begin and when does
it end?

If a counselee complains that he cannot understand the Bible, a
wise counselor will give some guidance but mainly will point out the
direction in which the counselee may find the answer. The understanding is not to be merely a mental understanding, but an applied
understanding. In fact, a person does not know the true meaning of
commands and principles in Scripture until he obeys them. For
instance, one may think he knows the meaning of love until he
begins meditating on 1 Corinthians 13. Then as he seeks to really
love he will learn more deeply the meaning of God's love. If a person
reads the Bible without doing what it says (particularly the instructions for living), the Word will be forgotten. But if he *does* what it
says he will remember and be transformed with the power of the
indwelling Holy Spirit.

As the Word is obeyed there is a coordination of spirit, soul,
and body so that there is peace even in the midst of turmoil. Also as
the Word is received and followed and the person walks after the
Spirit, he evidences fruit of the Spirit.

The counselor may suggest passages of Scripture that emphasize
aspects of the character of God. For instance, if a counselee needs
encouragement in faith, reading the biblical records of specific
incidents of God's faithfulness and meditating on God's promises to
be faithful can be very helpful. God instructed His people to remind,
themselves of His faithfulness and to teach their children about His
trustworthiness.

The Bible also serves as the primary weapon of spiritual warfare, particularly in the area of thoughts and desires.

> For the word of God is living and active and sharper than any two-edged sword, and piercing as far as the division of soul and spirit, of both joints and marrow, and able to judge the thoughts and intentions of the heart. (Hebrews 4:12)

Not only does the counselor need to know how to fight effectively with the Word of God; he needs to teach his counselee how to use this Sword of the Spirit to overcome fears, temptations, distortions, and lies of the archenemy of the soul. Only the truth of God can expose and defeat falsehood and bring about biblical changes in a person's life.

A counselor will not only use the Word of God for truth, wisdom, understanding, and healing within the counseling conversation but will teach the counselee how to find answers for his own problems from the Word. Once a counselee learns how to study the Bible, he will become "approved to God as a workman who does not need to be ashamed, handling accurately the word of truth" (2 Timothy 2:15). Rather than depending on the counselor for truth and insight, the counselee will learn how to find truth for himself in the Word through the revelation and application brought about by the Holy Spirit. Because of their dependence on the Lord for understanding and application of the Bible, both counselee and counselor need to pray for God's Word to be understandable to them as they read.

If a counselee is not able to concentrate on much reading at the beginning of counseling because of the possible overwhelming nature of the problem, the counselor may want to write out just a few verses on cards and ask the counselee to read, review, and think about them each day. Then as the counseling progresses, the amount and depth of Scripture can be increased as the Lord leads.

Although there are many good Christian books, these should not take precedence over the Bible. A few, however, which focus Scripture onto some solutions or new ways of thinking or acting and which would be particularly helpful for a counselee, may be recommended. The counselor should have read the book before suggesting it to a counselee. In fact, he may want to keep a record of books that would be useful for certain counselees. If it has been some time since he has read a particular book, the counselor should review it so he can discuss it intelligently. Also, he ought to keep in mind that not all people have the same capacity for reading, due to their interests, abilities, and educational backgrounds.

When Scripture has been assigned the counselor should take time during the next meeting to discuss the passages from the Bible and the understanding and application the counselee found during the week. This gives the counselee something positive to share and also helps the counselor determine what additional sections of Scripture to assign the next week. Also, discussing the passages encourages the counselee to read, meditate, and apply the Word during the week.

SPIRITUAL DIARY

For some people it is helpful to write a personal diary with the focus on the spiritual life. The writing should have a positive, faith-building direction rather than reams of complaining. For instance, a person could write down instances of God's faithfulness during the day. Or he could record the results of applying certain biblical principles. Or he could keep a record of God's dealings and what is being learned. Sometimes counselees record what is happening during the week to refresh their memories during the counseling time. The habit of writing down something about God's involvement in the person's daily life often reveals kindnesses of God that would otherwise be forgotten, unnoticed, or taken for granted.

As a person disciplines his mind to watch for evidence of the faithfulness of God in his life, and as a person disciplines himself into writing an account of God's involvement, he develops a tangible reminder of the loving constancy of God. Then when difficult times come at a later date, the person can refer back to the personal record of God's faithfulness. The diary is useful to center attention on God.

OTHER ACTIVITIES

Suggested activities will be as varied as the individuals who come in for counseling. As a counselor listens to the counselee and to the Lord, he will discern what changes in activity would be useful during the week. The assignment should meet the problem with specific applications of Scripture. The activity could be as simple as smiling, or it could involve serious areas of confession and repentance. It could be as practical as washing the floors or as artistic as writing a poem of praise. Most of the activities should include thinking and acting in order to develop a new habit or overcome a difficulty. The activity should uniquely fit the counselee.

Forms of artistic expression and participation can enhance faith for certain persons. Music reaches into the heart of most people in some form or another. A sensitive counselor will discover what kind of music, if any, might be helpful to a particular individual. There are numerous hymns that proclaim the truth and mercy of God. One person may benefit from listening to a recording and another person by memorizing and singing the hymn during the week.

Extending kindness to someone each day is also an excellent assignment for certain individuals. Just a card or a flower to a neighbor may express the love of God. As a counselee gives love to others and receives love from God he is participating in the exuberating flow of love. Sometimes a counselor may make suggestions, but it is better when the counselee thinks of ways to love those around him. In this way he begins to develop more sensitivity to the needs of others.

Physical exercise is a must for those who spend a great deal of time sitting. Caution would dictate, however, that a counselee should not suddenly take on a great deal of strenuous activity. Walking each day, consistently increasing the distance or speed, can have many beneficial results. The most obvious benefit is the exercise itself, but walking can also be valuable in giving a counselee the opportunity to contemplate the creativity and creation of God, meditate on His Word, or pray. Walking and breathing fresh air can have a positive effect on the emotions, also.

As a counselee is growing in the Lord, the activity can be exercising a gift of ministry. The Lord has given each person grace to minister. Though such ministry may begin by doing something for someone else, it may grow as the counselee discovers opportunities to be a blessing to those around him. He will also discover which ministering gifts he seems to have. An examination and discussion of the sections of Scripture dealing with gifts combined with a similar review of the kinds of activities of ministry the person seems to enjoy can be exciting and fruitful in the final stages of counseling.

DISCUSSING THE WEEK'S ACTIVITIES

After an assignment has been given the counselee, the discussion of activities during the next counseling session should include not only the successes of the counselee in completing the tasks, but also the failures. Christians can learn as much from their failures as from their successes if they are eager to learn from the Lord. For instance, if a person had agreed to smile every day, but only did it one day, he can be encouraged about the one day and perhaps compare the responses of those around him on that one day with what he usually experiences. The counselor also has to find out what activities are most helpful for a person and determine whether more or less should be given the next week.

Many times the changes through agreed-upon activities become the focus of a counseling session. Besides discussing these activities, the counselor may ask the counselee to share what he is gaining from involvement at other levels of church life—worship services, Bible studies, and friendships. At all times the Lord must be central in the activities themselves and in the discussions about the activities during the session. The purpose of activities and involvement in other areas of church life is to put into action the love of the Lord and to bring about actual changes each week so that the counselee is daily transformed into the image of the Lord Jesus Christ.

PART 4

Counseling in Your Church

16

Warnings

Many warnings could be sounded about biblical counseling, but we have limited this chapter to three which would be of help to those who are beginning a counseling ministry: the possible effect of distorted biblical doctrines; an amalgamation in so-called Christian healing; and the biological possibilities as underpinnings of mental-emotional-behavioral problems.

DISTORTED BIBLICAL DOCTRINES

A variety of so-called Christian practices are propagated as truth and applied to those who suffer from problems of living. The practitioners of these activities are often sincere but naive individuals who truly desire to help others through some new truth or technique found in a book, workshop, or tape. We have chosen to discuss only one of the several aberrations with which we are familiar. It is based upon a sound biblical teaching which has become generalized and applied without discernment.

Every Christian knows from Scripture about demons. The Bible teaches that individuals can become demonized and that demons are active in our world carrying out the work of their cruel master. One researcher reported a case of a transexual man who was completely delivered from his problem through the casting out of demons.[1]

1. Richard Restak, "The Sex-Change Conspiracy," *Psychology Today*, December 1979, p. 25.

Numerous beneficial deliverances could be reported to show that demons do exist and that they need to be cast out today just as in Jesus' day.

It is not our intention here, however, to discuss a doctrine of demons, but to warn about a distorted doctrine of demons. This distortion reduces all human problems to demon activity and all solutions to deliverance. It is easy to identify the kind of person who embraces this distorted doctrine because he is forever labeling human problems and diseases as demonic. If one is fearful, he calls it a demon of fear; if one is depressed, it is a demon of depression (or a spirit of depression); if one has asthma it is a demon or spirit of asthma. The disease is always a demon, and the treatment is always deliverance.

Each biblical counselor needs to be aware of demons and to be biblically sound in how to deal with them. There is a definite need for discernment of the Spirit. If this is not an area in which God has gifted an individual counselor, he should seek the guidance of his pastor. In addition to biblical understanding and the use of spiritual discernment no church counselor should move in this area (or any other area, for that matter) in contradiction to the leadership of the pastor and the teachings of his church. Spiritual counselors should not exist apart from a body of believers, and each counselor should know and follow the major teachings of his pastor and his church.

One final warning concerns the potential damage that may be inflicted by the malpractice of deliverance. We have had to deal with the results of the distorted application of this doctrine because damaged individuals have come to us for help. These persons have been told by the purveyors of deliverance that they had demons and needed deliverance. However, after various "deliverances" which included the usual "evidences" and activities of being delivered, no change occurred, thus leaving these individuals in a more desperate condition than before. One case involved a young woman who had a problem with depression. She was encouraged to see a religious healer who was well-known for his delusions of demons (he saw them in every case). After numerous repeated "deliverances" and "victories" she was just as depressed as ever. She concluded that she was infested with demons and that she was being destroyed from within. After "coming apart" she was admitted to the hospital, where it was determined that she had a biological problem related to the depression.

This one distorted doctrine of demons can cause real havoc in a counseling ministry and should be considered by any pastor who is setting up such a ministry. Although there are other distorted doctrines which can be detrimental, we have found that the distorted doctrine of demons can be the most devastating to a counseling ministry, because when people are desperate and deeply desire help they will reach out for almost anything available.

RELIGIOUS HEALING

Probably one of the most difficult areas to deal with is the amalgamation of the psychological with the spiritual offered as religious healing. There are numerous combinations which range from the innocent and innocuous to the deadly and disasterous. Many books, seminars, workshops, and speakers have altered the truth of Scripture by combining it with certain psychological systems.

In the last section we dealt with a sound biblical principle, deliverance from demons, taken to extremes. In this section we are considering a sound biblical doctrine which has been psychologized. There is a sound biblical inner healing. But most of the varieties with which we are familiar combine such psychological practices as scream therapy, rebirthing, resurrecting and reliving the past (including so-called prenatal traumas), and visual imagery.

Leaping into the past, plunging into the unconscious, conjuring up false images, and dramatizing all sorts of fantasies are the offerings of some inner healers. But an imaginary memory replaced by a fantasy only brings about imaginary healing. People need mental-emotional inner healing, but there is no need to concoct false images to replace real life experiences or a real past. Jesus said, "You shall know the truth, and the truth shall make you free." Dealing with the truth of our past, present, and future is the beginning of real inner healing.

All religious approaches that purport to heal memories and emotions or transform behavior and habits must be examined carefully in the light of Scripture. The Bible plus rebirthing or the Bible plus scream therapy or the Bible plus any other psychological gimmick must be avoided by the Christian.

There are many who began as biblical counselors and ended up with an amalgamation of truth (Bible) and error (psychological systems). The apostle John warns: "Beloved, do not believe every spirit, but test the spirits to see whether they are from God; because many false prophets have gone out into the world" (1 John 4:1). A biblical counseling ministry can be diminished and demolished by the amalgamation of the spiritual and the psychological.

BIOLOGICAL POSSIBILITIES

Some persons who come in for counseling are experiencing more than problems of living. Some have biological disturbances that affect the normal function of the brain and therefore are intricately involved with the person's thinking, feeling, and behaving. These individuals are an enigma even to the professionals, and they are often treated only with talk therapy when they actually require other kinds of help. There is also a disagreement among professionals as to how to treat such persons: with drugs, psychotherapy, electro-convulsive therapy, or a combination of these. Within this group, the biological involvement may escape detection, and endless psychotherapy may be administered with little, if any, progress. And, as a matter of fact, this is exactly what has happened to numerous individuals.[2] The biological involvement may be related to poor nutrition, inability to synthesize nutritional elements, lack of exercise, or far more complicated biological factors.

In *The Psychological Way/The Spiritual Way* we mention a number of physical diseases (such as general paresis, pellagrous psychosis, Parkinson's disease, hypoglycemia, and dystonia) which have been diagnosed as mental disorders. Wayne Sage reveals:

> Some psychiatrists once theorized that autistic children withdraw from affection because of cold, unloving parents and interpreted their bizarre behavior as symbolic of the resulting mental disturbance. Psychotherapeutic treatments did not prove effective, however, and sometimes even inflicted their own syndrome of guilt on parents.[3]

Numerous physical diseases not only have been but still are being treated by psychotherapy with little or no success and at great loss to those unfortunate enough to fall into this trap of treatment. Research psychiatrist Walter Reich says:

2. Martin Bobgan and Deidre Bobgan, *The Psychological Way/The Spiritual Way* (Minneapolis: Bethany Fellowship, 1979), chap. 9.
3. Wayne Sage, "Neurology Advances Understanding of Autism," *University of California Clip Sheet 56*, no. 13 (4 November 1980).

The psychiatry that has been familiar to America for the better part of the century has been pronounced "impractical, a failure, an embarrassment." The established professional approach . . . is rapidly being abandoned. And a new approach—a biological one, centered on the brain, on neurochemistry, on pharmacology, on medications—is rapidly gaining adherents.[4]

He continues, "The newer biological therapies have been shown to be more effective than purely psychological ones in their treatment."[5]

Through research and experimentation it has been shown that most kinds of severe mental disturbances are now thought to be biological in origin.[6] E. Fuller Torrey says, "Research evidence has become overwhelming that schizophrenia is truly a brain disease and involves abnormalities of both brain structure and function. Psychiatrists who state otherwise have probably been on a prolonged sabbatical to Tibet and subscribing only to *Popular Mechanics*."[7] Michael Thacher explains, "In schizophrenics, apparently, dopamine messengers run amuck, bombarding the mind with a flood of unrelated thoughts and feelings. The result is something like watching four T.V. channels simultaneously."[8] Psychiatrists Paul Wender and Donald Klein say,

> In facing the puzzle of mental illness, psychiatric savants of the first half of the twentieth century believed that Freudian theory would provide the answers. However, in the second half of the century, scientific research has uncovered evidence that biological malfunctions are central to mental illness and that much of the by now entrenched psychodynamic theory is irrelevant or even misleading.[9]

Wender and Klein explain:

> The lay public's resistance to medical treatment of psychiatric disorders comes from several directions. First, the middle and upper classes are suffering from cultural lag. Nurtured on psychoanalysis and sustained

4. Walter Reich, "Psychiatry's Second Coming," *Encounter* 57 (August 1981): 66.
5. Ibid., p. 71.
6. Robert Clairborne, "The Seeds of Insanity: Are They in the Genes?" *Science Digest*, March 1981, p. 30.
7. E. Fuller Torrey, Letter to Editor, *Psychology Today*, January 1981, p. 12.
8. Michael Thacher, "Creativity and Madness," *Human Behavior*, January 1979, p. 50.
9. Paul Wender and Donald Klein, "The Promise of Biological Psychiatry," *Psychology Today*, February 1981, pp. 25, 27.

by the promises of Gestalt therapy, transactional analysis, primal scream, and other therapies, they still believe that psychotherapy is the treatment of choice and that treatment with medication is inferior.[10]

As a biblical counselor works with an individual, he will want to determine whether the problems are mainly due to erroneous thinking and acting or if there might be some biological involvement. Because physical imbalances may either bring on or intensify emotional problems, a spiritual counselor needs to explore the general physical condition of anyone whom he is counseling. If there has been no physical examination within the prior year, he should suggest that the person have one. Additionally, it is wise for the counselor to determine the person's general nutritional pattern. If his diet is high in sugar, refined carbohydrates, caffeine, or alcohol there may be a definite link to his emotions and behavior. Some people become more nervous and angry when they eat too much sugar; others become more depressed.[11]

Even though a spiritual counselor may not know much about drugs and medication, it is wise to inquire whether or not a person who is in for counseling is taking any drugs and to become familiar with any that are being used. Inexpensive paperbacks are available which list the variety of pills and their known effects.

Counselors should not recommend that a counselee stop or start taking medication. Such recommendations can only be made by a medical doctor. It is unwise to make a person feel guilty about taking medication. Many people feel that they are failures if they are regularly taking any kind of pills, yet chemicals, such as thyroid or insulin, are essential to maintain a chemical or hormone balance in the body. Others may be taking chemicals that balance the emotional states without dulling the brain, such as lithium. Many others, however, are in bondage to tranquilizers that only dull the emotions without bringing any solutions. It would be foolish to encourage a person to quit taking insulin or lithium, but as a counselee develops more satisfactory means of meeting with difficult circumstances or emotional stress, he may be able to cut down on tranquilizer types of drugs. In either case, drug usage should be only under the direction of a physician.

10. Ibid., p. 41.
11. Sydney Walker III, "Blood Sugar and Emotional Storms," *Psychology Today*, July 1975, p. 74.

It is good to be aware of the possible biological involvement in certain disorders. If there is any suspicion of biological problems a counselee should be referred to a medical doctor. However, it should be noted that because the pendulum has swung toward medication for mental disturbances, many medical doctors are prescribing drugs at the drop of a hat. People experiencing divorce, separation, loss of a job, or other life traumas are often too easily given drugs to relieve the hardships of those incidents. Reich reports that there has been a dramatic rise in the past twenty years of prescriptions for antidepressant medication, antipsychotic agents, and minor tranquilizers. [12]

We want to make it clear that we are neither recommending nor discouraging the use of drugs for mental disorders. Our purpose is to bring more awareness in the realm of possible biological involvement and also to show that the image of psychological counseling is becoming more tarnished in that it has unfortunately been used for biological diseases with little or no success, but always at great expense. In addition, we want to explode the myth that psychotherapy is the answer to extreme mental disorders.

Exercise and sleep affect the mental-emotional state of a person. Exercise that builds the cardiovascular system enables the person to supply blood and oxygen to the brain more efficiently. Lack of sleep and normal dream patterns may also lead to emotional distress. One way to break down a person emotionally is to prevent him from sleeping or dreaming over an extended period of time. Some researchers believe that the brain regains its chemical balance through dreaming. And we all know from experience how much worse we are emotionally and mentally when we have been deprived of sleep.

Good nutrition and natural means of healing can be encouraged. A biblical counselor needs to become aware of basic principles of nutrition, not going overboard with fads, but maintaining sensible standards, which include eating from the basic food groups, cutting down on empty calories, and using healthful food preparation. Again, the counselor would not prescribe specific vitamins, minerals, or herbs, because this would be practicing in the health sciences. General information may be given as well as encouragement. Even more important than the food we eat, however, is the frame of mind of the person while he is eating.

12. Reich, p. 68.

Counseling individuals with possible biological involvement can be an area of weakness for both the psychological counselor and the church. The psychological counselor tends to view problems as solely psychologically based, and the spiritual counselor may see problems as solely spiritual. Neither counseling the psychological way nor ministering the spiritual way will be the complete answer for certain persons. But one who ministers according to Scripture has more to offer in guidance and wisdom to one who is suffering mental-emotional disturbances related to physical disorders than the psychological counselor because of prayer, the support of the Body of Christ, and the involvement of God in the counseling process.

17

A Plan for Counseling in Your Church

Each body of believers that desires to develop a counseling ministry should do so on the basis of scriptural guidelines and within the existing church structure. This section is merely to suggest ways to develop and conduct a counseling ministry. Some of the suggestions may not be practical in every church, but the framework may provide a starting place.

Biblical counseling should be under the authority of the local church body and accountable to the leadership of the church. Each counselor should be in submission to the Lord, the leadership, and the Body of Christ. Counselors should be appointed and designated by the leadership to serve the Lord by ministering to those in the congregation who are suffering from problems of living. Because of the heavy reliance on the Holy Spirit and because counseling is a function of the Body of Christ and an expression of the love of God, there should be no fee. Ideally, counseling should be a natural outflow of love and ministry in a fellowship of believers who know and love one another. Counseling may arise out of a relationship of trust already established between a leader and member of a small-group ministry in a church.

The biblical counseling ministry at our church grew out of a need in the body. Our pastor was becoming overburdened with the heavy load of counseling and yet felt the responsibility to minister to the flock. He began calling on some of us in the congregation to share this load and to meet with various individuals who were experiencing problems of living. As we became more involved, we saw this as a ministry which the Lord desired for His people—a function of the Body of Christ.

In Genesis, Jethro suggested a similar plan to Moses. Day after day the people lined up outside the tent of Moses to seek counsel and advice, just as many in the church may come to the pastor for counsel. Jethro could see that this was too overwhelming a task for one man to accomplish and suggested that Moses share this responsibility with others. Moses assigned leaders of groups and taught them the ways of God so that they could counsel those who needed to know God's way in a particular situation and to find God's solutions to problems. Far more ministry is needed in the Body of Christ than one person can meet singlehandedly. Kevin Springer of *Pastoral Renewal* is concerned that "many leaders spend long, difficult hours with a minority of their people, only to see the more gifted, mature members neglected—precisely the members who could be equipped to serve others themselves."[1] A wise pastor will lead others into areas of shared ministry so that the whole body may function together and thus express the wholeness and holiness intended by the Lord of the church.

It is extremely helpful when a pastor can refer an individual to a biblical counselor within the local fellowship so that the person in need does not fall into the hands of "self-appointed counselors" or have to turn to those outside the church who might counsel according to philosophies and teachings not in agreement with the teachings of the fellowship. No place in Scripture says to send an individual out into the world to find help for problems of living. Jesus called His disciples to minister, and He sent His Holy Spirit to meet the needs of the people.

DEVELOPING A COUNSELING MINISTRY

The basic elements for change already exist within a church in which there is an environment of love and in which there is sound teaching of the Word. Biblical counseling in the church is just a more personal and specific form of ministering the mercy and truth of God. Therefore, biblical counseling should not appear foreign. And

1. Keven N. Springer, "Counsel, Administrate, and Give Sermons to the Flock?" *Pastoral Renewal* 6, no. 9 (March 1982): 69.

yet, many ministers and lay people feel totally unequipped because they think that biblical counseling somehow has to emulate psychological counseling.

Biblical counseling involves the fellowship of love in the body (the environment for change) and the preaching and teaching of the Word (direction for change) rather than techniques and theories of psychological counseling.

When a pastor desires to develop a counseling ministry within the body, he needs to turn more attention to individualizing what is already happening within the group. In biblical counseling the caring becomes personal through giving time and listening, and the teaching becomes personal to meet the specific needs of the individual. Thus the environment and direction for change through the giving of mercy and truth are adapted to one person rather than to an entire group. The pastor has more to give than he may realize.

Members of the congregation may also have more to give in counseling than they realize. As they have participated as members of a caring environment, and as they have personally followed the truths of Scripture in their own lives, they have experienced the effects of a loving environment and of direction for change. Many have already provided that environment of mercy and direction for change through personal interaction with other Christians. Thus many are already equipped to serve in the capacity of biblical counselor.

Unless a congregation contains only new or very young believers, there is a group of individuals in the fellowship who are equipped to counsel. These persons already have studied the Bible and have applied the Word in their own lives. They have the gift of counseling with a balance of mercy and truth. All congregations that we have been in touch with regarding a counseling ministry have individuals who are willing and able to minister immediately if the opportunity were given. Setting up a counseling ministry is merely a matter of selecting counselors, giving those counselors training in basic principles they will need to apply in their counseling, organizing and announcing the ministry, and trusting God for the results.

In addition to the training from the Lord they have already received, counselors and prospective counselors continue to learn as they search the Scriptures for God's ways of ministering to people, as they read books to gain from the experience of others who counsel according to the Word, and then as they actually begin to minister to

individuals. The greatest way to learn how to do something is to do
it. Guidelines are necessary, but the only way to really learn is to
begin providing the environment of mercy through listening, caring,
and praying. Then as the Holy Spirit gives wisdom, the teaching is
added. Reliance on the Holy Spirit cannot be overemphasized,
because the best environment for counseling comes from God's
presence and the direction for change comes from His Word as it is
made applicable and living by the Holy Spirit.

One of the most seemingly awesome aspects of beginning a
counseling ministry is the training program. Many pastors feel
inadequate to teach a class in biblical counseling. Yet they have been
preaching and teaching from the pulpit the same biblical principles
that are foundational to biblical counseling. Since a biblical counselor ministers through mercy and truth to provide an environment
for change and direction for change, the training should be in those
two areas.

Teaching about providing an environment of mercy will certainly be familiar to a minister who has encouraged that kind of
environment within his congregation. Since he will normally have
been teaching about love, kindness, mercy, patience, longsuffering,
understanding, and other qualities that should be developing as the
fruit of the Spirit, he will already have a wealth of materials from
which to draw.

Additionally, he should select lay counselors who already
exhibit such qualities and fruit of the Spirit. The teaching in this area
may then be supplemented with articles and books that stress the
care of one another in the Body of Christ.

A minister is also familiar with training counselors to provide
direction within the counseling setting. He will be teaching counselors what to teach, and that will be how to live the Christian life. He
will be teaching them to personalize the same kind of teaching of the
Word that he does from the pulpit; how to live the Christian life
through receiving God's love, believing Him, and obeying Him.

Since preaching, group teaching, and individual counseling all
include instruction in how to live the Christian life and other
foundational doctrines of Scripture, it is interesting to look at some
of the similarities and differences. Biblical preaching, teaching, and
counseling should: (1) be based on the doctrines of Scripture; (2) be
centered on God and His character, Word, and will; (3) guide
persons in how to live the Christian life; (4) motivate people to

choose and do God's will; (5) exhort, explain, encourage, and love; (6) be dependent upon the Holy Spirit; (7) identify the needs of the persons listening; and (8) nurture healing, change, and growth.

There are ways in which counseling differs from preaching or teaching a group. The manner of presentation in counseling includes listening as well as speaking. Both the counselee and counselor learn about each other as well as about the Lord. What is taught is based on individual need as discerned through listening and through prayer, whereas in teaching or preaching the topic is based on group needs as discerned through getting to know the group and through prayer. At times counseling may be that personal contact of mercy while a counselee is choosing the Lord's direction. Probably the differences could be summed up in these words: counseling is more personal, happens through conversation, touches specific needs, and extends the mercy and truth of God through time given to one person or couple.

The same truths can be taught from the pulpit, in the classroom, and during counseling. Therefore, a minister can do much to train his own people in biblical counseling. But, counseling itself is a different gift from preaching and teaching. Quite often a minister who is highly gifted in the pulpit and who can therefore teach much about counseling may not actually have the gift of counseling. Conversely, there are people who have the interpersonal qualities and the ability to listen with great understanding and patience who are able to counsel effectively, but who would put an audience to sleep. The source of mercy and truth is the same, but the gift, the calling, and the manner of presentation are different. Therefore, even a minister who does not see himself as a counselor can be instrumental in teaching others much of what they need to know for counseling.

SETTING UP A COUNSELING MINISTRY

1. *Legalities.* Most states regulate and license psychological counselors. But as long as there are no fees charged and it is clear that what is being performed is not psychological counseling, biblical counseling will not be in violation of regulations concerning such secular practices. Biblical counseling is under the umbrella of pastoral counseling and is a religious function protected by the First Amendment of the Constitution of the United States. Even so, in our

culture, lawsuits are common, and churches may wish to consider increasing insurance to cover any possibility of litigation.

2. *Initial planning.* Through prayer and discussion the leadership of the church may determine the need of the local body. The pastor generally has a pretty good idea how many people in the congregation could benefit from such a ministry. The pastor and lay leaders should determine personal qualifications for counselors and select them accordingly. They should, together with the counselors, select materials for study, decide the extent of the ministry, and determine guidelines.

3. *Educational training.* Because the Bible is the primary source book for biblical counseling, the ongoing Bible classes and sermons provide a basis for training counselors. Those Bible classes and sermons which bring forth the application of the Word of God in a person's life are the most useful for biblical counselors. If the pastor desires to offer any special training, he should only use those materials which are in agreement with Scripture, such as those written by Jay Adams. Quite often a church will turn to professional psychological counselors for training biblical counselors, but we would advise that they not do so. If church leaders choose psychological training they will end up with something other than biblical counseling.

4. *Selecting counselors.* The pastor and leaders of the church may designate certain individuals to be biblical counselors in the church. They would be the persons to whom the pastor would refer those seeking help. The following list of characteristics of a biblical counselor may assist in selecting counselors:

a. A believer who has a saving knowledge of the Lord Jesus Christ and who is living under His Lordship (following His teachings and commandments).

b. A mature believer, one who has known the Lord and relied upon the indwelling Holy Spirit for some time. One who has allowed the Lord Jesus to be formed in him.

c. A believer who knows the Bible well, who knows how to apply the Scriptures in his own life, and who will counsel according to the Bible. Unless a counselor knows the Bible, he will counsel from worldly knowledge and experience.

d. A believer who is sound in doctrine and in agreement with the church's statement of faith.

e. A believer who is teachable and under submission to the pastor and the Body of Christ.

f. A believer who is loyal to Jesus, the local church, and the pastor.

g. A believer who has shown consistency, dependability, and responsibility in other work in the church.

h. A believer who is able to keep confidences.

i. A believer who is able to listen, to love, and to teach; one who is gifted in maintaining the balance of exhortation, teaching, and mercy, according to Romans 12.

j. A believer whom others respect and seek out for counsel and friendship.

k. A believer who follows his or her scriptural role in the home and whose own house is in order. If a counselor is experiencing too many problems of his own, he will not be able to adequately bear the burdens of others in counseling.

l. A believer who relies on the Holy Spirit and who is faithful to pray for those he counsels; one who believes that God guides and directs His children and answers prayer.

m. A believer who manifests the fruit of the Spirit, especially love, patience, gentleness, and meekness.

n. A believer who does not intimidate, manipulate, or control others.

o. A believer who will not encourage those he counsels to become dependent on him.

5. *Who counsels whom.* The pastor and church leaders also need to formulate guidelines on matching counselor with counselee. Although pastors may counsel all persons, we suggest that men counsel men, women counsel women, and couples minister to couples. Additionally, age variables should be considered. The counselor should have the maturity necessary to counsel a particular individual. It is usually best for the counselor to be close in age or older than the counselee, although that is not always necessary. Also, the counselor should have experienced being a parent if he is to counsel others in parenting, not only for the knowledge gained through experience but also for the humility that comes with experience. Because of the need for similarities in age, older

members of the congregation can be very helpful in the counseling ministry. On the other hand, a teenager who is struggling with problems may best be ministered to by a young adult who has the maturity to guide the counselee in the right direction.

Cultural and educational backgrounds may also contribute to whether or not the counseling is helpful. It is very easy to assume that just because we live in the same country we have the same cultural backgrounds. But certain values are more prominant in some backgrounds than in others. Also, a person who is highly educated may not be receptive to being counseled by someone of lesser education even though the counselor has a great deal to give. This cannot be a firm rule either, since those people who do not tend to intellectualize along with their counselees may be more effective because they move truth into the arena of living instead of keeping doctrine at a safe distance from the heart, feet, and hands. Thus, although background differences need to be considered, other factors may be more important for the counseling to move in the right direction.

6. *Counseling load.* Because biblical counseling is a shared ministry, each counselor should minister to a limited number of individuals. Professional counselors have to fill their appointment calendar in order to generate a professional income. Therefore one of the doctrines of the professionals is this: Do not become emotionally involved with your clients. And no wonder! Can you imagine the emotional drain that would occur if the professional counselor became emotionally involved with forty different clients to the extent that he thought about them, prayed for them, and felt concern for them beyond the appointment time and beyond the time spent writing up reports? Romans 12:10-15 tells the biblical counselor something different: Be involved.

> Be devoted to one another in brotherly love; give preference to one another in honor; not lagging behind in diligence, fervent in spirit, serving the Lord; rejoicing in hope, persevering in tribulation, devoted to prayer, contributing to the needs of the saints, practicing hospitality. . . . Rejoice with those who rejoice, and weep with those who weep. (Romans 12:10-13, 15)

In the Body of Christ we are called to love one another, and in many instances love takes time, particularly when the person being loved is going through the pain of problems of living. If a biblical counselor has too large a load he cannot be as available to a counselee as when he limits the number of counselees. A counselor who is ministering to a person who is suicidal should not be loaded down with many other counselees. On the other hand, if a counselor is ministering to people who are growing through their problems and do not require as much time, that counselor may increase his load.

A counselor needs to have the time to meet regularly with the Lord in prayer and in the Word. He needs to fellowship with the Lord and feed on His Word so that he does not become a dried up well. Only as a biblical counselor is receiving the water of life from the Lord can he give water to those who thirst. A biblical counselor also needs to have the time to be fellowshiping with the body. Some church workers suffer from the burnout syndrome similar to those in the secular helping professions if they only give and do not use their time to receive from the Lord.

7. *Counselors and friends.* Some people would rather bare their soul to a complete stranger with whom they will not have social contact. They fear exposure to people with whom they regularly come in contact for several reasons. They may feel as though the one who has served as counselor and who knows their secrets will socially relate to them according to those secrets. Also, they may feel exposed around the person in social situations just because of the private nature of counseling. On the other hand, many people share their deepest thoughts and concerns with their closest friends and do not fear that the friends will treat them differently because of the confession. The love that is expressed in a relationship of commitment laced with mercy, forgiveness, understanding, gentleness, and protection makes the difference. If the counseling relationship is clinical or if the counselor is in a position higher than the counselee, then social contact may be feared. But if a real friendship has developed between the one who counsels and the one being counseled, and if a strong communication of acceptance and security has been established, then the counselee should feel secure in social situations in which the counselor is present.

People who hold responsible positions in a fellowship may be reluctant to share spiritual shortcomings and failures of relationship with a person of the same fellowship. And yet that is exactly what James exhorts believers to do: "Therefore, confess your sins to one another, and pray for one another, so that you may be healed. The

effective prayer of a righteous man can accomplish much" (James
5:16). A counselor who has honestly faced the depravity of his own
flesh will not have a critical or self-righteous attitude. Rather, he will
stand as a brother and a friend to the one who is experiencing
problems of living. Proverbs speaks of friendship as it relates to
counseling:

> A friend loves at all times,
> and a brother is born for adversity.
> > (Proverbs 17:17)

> Faithful are the wounds of a friend,
> but deceitful are the kisses of an enemy.
> > (Proverbs 27:6)

> Oil and perfume make the heart glad,
> So a man's counsel is sweet to his friend.
> > (Proverbs 27:9)

> Iron sharpens iron;
> so one man sharpens another.
> > (Proverbs 27:17)

Biblical counseling and Christian friendship are quite similar. Both
should follow Jesus' command to love one another as He loves us.
Both call believers to bear one another's burdens and to build up one
another in the faith. The conversation of both counseling and
friendship should include listening in mercy and truth, responding
with understanding, speaking the mercy and truth that will best edify
the other person, and encouraging growth in Christian maturity.

The same things that can ruin friendship can ruin counseling: a
superior attitude, self-righteousness, a know-it-all attitude, unforgiveness, possessiveness, bossiness, an authoritarian attitude, eager-
ness to give advice, disappointment with the other, revealing of
secrets, and lack of acceptance. A true friend or counselor will bring
out the best in a person through the exercise of mercy and truth.

8. *Keeping confidences.* Guidelines for keeping confidences also
need to be established. A counselor will be very careful to keep
confidences, but may occasionally need to share a concern with the
pastor for the greatest benefit to the counselee. There are numerous
admonitions in Scripture not to spread tales.

9. *A place for counseling.* A place for counseling is an important consideration. In most instances of biblical counseling privacy is essential. Therefore, designated rooms in the church building are ideal. The church is common ground, and it is a place to do business with God. It is the place where Christians meet to worship, pray, and hear the Word. Therefore, it is the logical place for counseling.

10. *Intake and appointment procedure.* Counseling intake and appointment procedures may be set up in numerous ways. It is best to have one person coordinate the initial arrangements. When an individual indicates a need for counseling, the pastor or church secretary may ask that person to call the counseling coordinator. The coordinator may then give a brief description of the counseling ministry so that the prospective counselee will not be expecting something different from what is available. The coordinator should explain that this is a lay counseling ministry and not professional psychological counseling, that there is no fee, and that it is available to persons in the congregation or to persons who do not have a church home who are willing to attend services.

If the individual is interested in obtaining counsel, the coordinator may obtain such pertinent information as name, telephone number, times when the person can be reached, type of counseling requested (personal, marriage, family), the general nature of the problem, approximate age, and similar information about immediate family members if applicable. The coordinator will then locate a counselor. From then on all appointments may be made personally between the counselee and counselor, though if a room in the church is used, the counselor should check first to see that it will be available.

11. *Record-keeping.* The coordinator's records can be very basic and include the information received on the first phone call, along with the date and the assigned counselor's name. The coordinator may add other information, such as duration of counseling, names and ages of children (if any), and any other information that might be helpful. The counselor may wish to keep a record of appointment times with brief notes and assignments that have been given. Such records should be kept private and should not reveal details of too confidential a nature.

12. *Review of counseling activities.* As a biblical counselor ministers in mercy and truth he will be engaged in a number of activities. It is helpful to review on a regular basis a list such as the one that

follows to be sure that the counseling is balanced. Such a review will also remind counselors of activities they may have forgotten to include with particular counselees. Biblical counseling involves the following:

a. Remembering that the purpose of counseling is spiritual growth as well as solving problems (Colossians 1:28).

b. Actively learning and growing in your own walk with the Lord.

c. Cooperating with God's creative process of transforming the counselee through the renewing of the mind (Romans 12:1-2).

d. Listening to communicate love and concern and to understand the person and the nature of his problem.

e. Teaching, which includes correction and training as well as communicating God's ways (2 Timothy 3:16-4:4).

f. Loving and accepting the individual as a person of value to the Lord (John 15:12).

g. Edifying, which includes building up the person in the Lord, bolstering his faith and confidence in God, and enlarging his concept of the Lord (Ephesians 4:12, 16, 29).

h. Counseling, advising, or suggesting a policy or plan of action or behavior, according to biblical principles.

i. Suggesting ways to apply Scripture to circumstances (2 Timothy 3:16-17).

j. Exercising patience, for problems that have developed and persisted for years may take time to heal (Ephesians 4:1-2).

k. Trusting God for the real work of healing and transforming.

l. Encouraging the counselee to cooperate with God in the healing process.

m. Being objective without losing the grace of compassion.

n. Determining the area of growth within God's plan and timing for the particular counselee.

o. Comforting the person in pain; strengthening and giving hope with comfort to ease the grief or trouble of an individual, but watching out for the danger of too much sympathy; not commiserating with or pitying a person who is pining under his circumstances (2 Corinthians 1:4).

p. Seeing spiritual goals for the counselee and helping him to move toward those goals without imposing a form of legalism.

q. Maintaining an attitude of humility.

r. Praying with consistency and persistence.

s. Believing God's promises and His faithfulness to overcome the temptation of discouragement.

t. Giving all of the credit and glory to God for His work of transforming a counselee.

As a counselor continues to minister according to the Word of God he will discover other activities he will want to add to this list.

13. *Counselor evaluation.* Although the focus of the counselor is on God and His Word and His ways of ministering truth and mercy, and although careful attention is given to the counselee's words and needs, a counselor must also pay attention to his own attitudes and activities within the counseling session. One way for a counselor to prevent himself from becoming careless or lopsided in his counseling is to seek God about the following questions:

a. Am I getting too involved in the problem, or am I seeing beyond the problem to God's ability and to God's alternatives?

b. Am I casting blame, or am I bringing clarity and forgiveness?

c. Am I excusing sin or allowing the Holy Spirit to pinpoint what needs to be changed?

d. Am I offering the comfort of God or commiserating in pity?

e. Am I fearful of what a counselee might do (such as commit suicide), or do I balance caution with trust in God?

f. Am I following the guidance of God's Word and the Holy Spirit, or am I becoming manipulated through emotions, flattery, or guilt induction?

g. Am I either listening too much or talking too much?

h. Am I helping the counselee to become dependent on God or on me?

i. Am I exercising partiality or staying objective when there is conflict between two persons?

j. Am I relying on my own ideas and advice, or am I finding answers from God's Word?

k. Am I ministering in the attitude of humility or do I feel a bit superior to the counselee?

l. Am I finding that I am developing a critical attitude toward a counselee?

m. How much responsibility am I taking for the counselee's actions before, during, or after a counseling session?

n. Am I becoming discouraged, or am I developing patience?

o. Am I blaming myself when there is little progress or congratulating myself when things are going well?

p. Am I becoming dogmatic and overbearing, or am I being gentle and kind?

q. Am I praying consistently for the counselee and for wisdom from the Lord?

r. Am I giving principles without suggestions for application?

s. Am I loving the counselee as Jesus would have me love him?

14. *Duration and frequency of counseling.* The duration and frequency of counseling will vary from person to person. The counselor will want to meet often enough and long enough to see change and growth or at least some problems resolved. Yet the counseling relationship should not continue as an ongoing form of dependency. Nor should it exceed the time the counselee wants to meet. A church may wish to establish guidelines to limit counseling to a maximum period of time. However, the guidelines would have to be somewhat flexible.

The usual pattern is to meet weekly at the beginning unless the nature of the problem warrants more frequency. A week's interval gives the counselee time to practice what has been suggested in counseling. When it looks as though the counselee is equipped to move on, it is sometimes wise to lengthen the time between appointments to two weeks and then to three weeks for a few more visits. Also, a counselee may want to talk with the counselor at infrequent intervals to review new patterns or discuss new problems. Because a friendship is established in biblical counseling, there will probably be many times the two will see one another at church and talk briefly.

15. *When to stop counseling.* Biblical counseling provides the person-to-person listening and teaching that believers need during

certain periods of growth and especially during times of need. Within the caring and teaching environment of a body of believers, a person does not need to be counseled until all problems are resolved or until he has reached some high level of spiritual growth, particularly if he is involved in a small-group ministry. Some persons may need to continue counseling for several months, and others find that only a few times of meeting are necessary. The possibilities for growth do not terminate after counseling because of the ongoing ministry within the body of believers.

The happiest and most positive culminations for counseling are those in which goals have been at least partially reached and those in which the counselees have grown closer to the Lord in relationship, trust, and obedience. Other positive endings are when persons are heading in the right direction and are able to move on within the group ministries.

On the other hand, there are times when a person discontinues biblical counseling because that person has chosen to go a different direction. Also, there are times when a counselor sees that progress is not being made or that the counselee is resistant to the counseling. In that case, the counselor would discuss the situation with the pastor or lay person who directs the counseling ministry. At that time they could pray about whether the counselee would be better off with another counselor, without counseling for awhile, or with a small group. There are times when church discipline is necessary, and one should follow the procedure of Matthew 18.

A counselor may express the kindness and mercy of God, may point the way, and encourage. But the choice to follow the Lord belongs to the counselee. If there is resistance of will against trusting the Lord and an implied or stated threat that the counselor must not point out the truth, it is really best to discontinue counseling. Such a decision cannot be made hastily after only a few sessions, however, because time needs to be given for a relationship of trust to develop. Also, the counselor needs to determine whether or not the resistance comes from fear, in which case more mercy and teaching about the Lord's grace would be in order rather than termination.

When discontinuing counseling, the counselor needs to continue to act in mercy and love and to keep the door open for future possibilities. The counselor may do that by saying that biblical counseling is heading in one direction, and that is to follow Jesus and to obey Him. It involves putting off the old ways and putting on new ones. It involves changing thinking and behavior according to God's best for the person. Counseling involves change, not just talking and listening. If the counselee is looking for something other than that, then perhaps he might want to discontinue.

Even at a point of ending counseling before changes have been made or problems resolved, the counselor should not make the counselee feel that he has failed, but rather that perhaps he is not ready for counseling at that time. The counselor should encourage the counselee to continue in the worship, fellowship, and teaching in the body of believers. Persons who are not necessarily receptive to counseling should not be abandoned. They should be accepted as persons, and they should be encouraged to avail themselves of other groups and ministries in the church. And, above all, a biblical counselor should continue to care and pray for the counselee even after counseling has ended.

16. *Referral within the body.* Sometimes a counselee and counselor do not work well together in counseling. Several factors may bring about such difficulty. The two persons simply may not be compatible because of their personality qualities. That does not mean that the counselee cannot be counseled or that the counselor should not be counseling. Rather, it indicates that a better pairing of counseling partners could be made. Some counselees work best with a counselor who is strong in mercy but not as strong in exhortation. Others seem to progress better with counselors especially gifted in exhortation and encouragement. The factors that brought about the mismatch may also have to do with upbringing, social customs, educational background, and even ethnic differences.

If a counselee or counselor thinks that it would be better to change partners for counseling, neither should be made to feel that he has failed in any way. Counseling is much like friendship. Certain people are drawn together as close friends. Others may care about one another in the Body of Christ but not be drawn together in the same closeness. Because counseling is much like biblical friendship, there needs to be a compatibility of personalities and a sense of appreciation for each other.

Also, there are times when a counselor and counselee work together quite well, but the counselor believes that another person in the body could minister better to a particular problem area. When a counselor discovers various needs of the individual, he can draw upon other members of the body who can minister through the gifts of mercy and helps or through experiences of living. Furthermore, a counselor will encourage friend relationships and participation in a small group within the body.

17. *Referral outside of the body.* Almost every book written on counseling from a Christian perspective in the past twenty-five years recommends, at some point of difficulty, referring individuals who are suffering from problems of living to a community psychotherapist. As we have shown earlier, research does not support such referrals. People who are suffering from the ordinary problems of living are generally more satisfied with nonprofessional than professional help, and no one has shown conclusively that results produced by professionals are better than those produced by nonprofessionals.

The counseling staff at our church deals with the full range of problems of living. The counseling is from a biblical perspective and relies upon biblical means of change. During the entire time in which we have codirected the ministry, no one has been referred to a psychotherapist of any kind, Christian or otherwise. For problems of living that can be dealt with through a form of talk therapy, we believe that biblical counseling is the preferable form of counseling.

Yet, as we noted in chapter 16, there are individuals for whom talking is not enough. They have biological problems that affect their emotions and even prevent them from thinking coherently. They may experience large swings in the emotions, deep depression, hallucinations, or uncontrollable behavior, and they do need medical help. Spiritual counseling can supplement that medical treatment, but it cannot replace it. Most people refer such individuals to professional psychologists and psychiatrists, who perform psychological counseling, when the counselees really need medical, biological help. It is true that because psychiatrists are medical doctors they can prescribe the medicine that is necessary in these cases, but all too often they will pursue psychological means of treating the patient rather than (or along with) biochemical therapy. Therefore, in our counseling ministry we do not refer people with emotional problems of biochemical origin to psychologists. Instead, we refer them to medical doctors for treatment. The treatment the doctor gives is supplemented with spiritual counseling.

18. *Suicide.* Threats of suicide are extremely frightening because of the possibility that the person making such a threat will

actually kill himself. No threat of suicide can be taken lightly or ignored even though such threats may be manipulative devices or may not be carried out. Many people who contemplate suicide have lost hope for relief or change or are crying out for somebody to help them.

If a person is suicidal, more than one person needs to be alerted and involved. Because of the serious nature of suicidal threats and the possible biological involvement, a person who is suicidal should also be under the care of a medical doctor—not for psychological counseling but for medical diagnosis and possible biological treatment. If any form of talk therapy (counseling) can help the suicidal individual, the church has more to give than a psychological counselor. Furthermore, within the structure of the church there should be a network of available persons to visit, phone, and pray for this person. The church has more time, availability, love, and help to give a suicidal individual than one lonely, fifty-minute-per-week psychotherapist. The church is one body composed of enough people for around-the-clock availability when necessary. One minister cannot be available for so many hours, but when the responsibility is shared by the body there can be a strong supportive network of love. Furthermore, while some are ministering directly, others can be praying.

19. *What about Christian psychotherapists?* A great deal of confidence has been placed in those who refer to themselves as Christian psychologists. The reason for this confidence is that such psychologists say that they merge professional training with a Christian world view. On the surface this combination looks perfect; however, the type of amalgamation and the extent of amalgamation may not remain true to the Word of God. A minister does not know the actual mixture of the psychological way with the spiritual way by which a particular Christian psychotherapist counsels. In fact, a Christian who practices psychotherapy may involve nothing of Christianity except a similar moral code. One local Christian psychotherapist to whom ministers refer their flock not only does not amalgamate the biblical way with the psychological way, but even refuses to pray with a believer upon request. He counsels strictly by the models and methods of psychotherapy.

No matter how personable and well-meaning a Christian psychotherapist may be, he can easily be so heavily influenced by the theories and techniques of the psychological way that these eclipse the biblical truths that are basic to walking in the spirit rather than walking in the flesh. His real dependence for counseling may be not in the Bible but in his training and techniques, and he may actually be promoting teachings that feed the flesh rather than the spirit. Jesus plus Freud (psychoanalysis) or Jesus plus Janov (primal scream) or Jesus plus Berne and Harris (transactional analysis) does not equal the Bible. Nor does the Freudian therapy that encourages searching through and reexperiencing the past in order to find self-understanding. Instead, such counseling actually focuses more on self than on Jesus, who alone offers the way out.

Yet though the counseling may focus more on self than on Jesus, because the counselor is labeled a Christian psychologist, the counselee may be even less likely to see the faults of the counseling than he would if the counselor were not a Christian. That is because there is a tendency to make psychological ideas sound all right when a Christian psychologist says them, as though a person labeled *Christian psychologist* is always going to say and do what is Christian. Thus the added confidence and status of one who is both a *Christian* (knows the way of God) and a *psychologist* (understands and can help people) may actually encourage greater gullibility on the part of the counselee to whatever the counselor says, whether it is biblically sound or not.

In addition, no matter whether professional psychotherapy is conducted by a Christian or not, it still operates on a frantic schedule of one counseling session after another, with up to fifty appointments held in a given week. No such system, whether it is provided by a Christian or a non-Christian, can be very beneficial to the recipient.

There are no doubt Christian therapists who have discarded much of what they have learned from secular theories and therapies, but we have found personally that we can fool ourselves into thinking that we have abandoned the psychological way when we are actually still thinking according to the ideas of men promoted by those systems. In order to move from psychological training to ministering the way of the Lord, the therapist must spend much time in the Word and in prayer. He will need knowledge of the Word and the guidance of the Holy Spirit in determining what observations from any field, included psychology, are correct. Lastly, though he will not want to close his eyes to facts accurately observed and reported by psychologists and others about human nature, he will have to make a conscious decision to discard the psychological way of thinking and counseling if he is to move successfully beyond it.

20. *Will biblical counseling help all people?* Measuring the results of biblical counseling is at least as subjective as the attempts to determine whether or not psychological counseling works. However, if we look at the most intensive form of discipleship (which is really what much of biblical counseling is about) we do not find a 100 percent improvement rate. Even though Jesus ministered truth in mercy to His chosen twelve and led them into the deeper truths of the spiritual life and empowered them with authority over demons and diseases, there was one who was not transformed. Judas did not benefit or grow from the love poured into him or from the revelation of truth. He not only rejected the teachings, but he turned against the One who was about to die for his sins. In fact, Judas even committed suicide—after three years with Jesus. Can one say that Jesus' ministry was inadequate because Judas was not changed? Can one say that Judas's suicide was a result of some failure in Jesus' ministry?

There will be people in the church who want help but who do not actually want the full scope of Christianity. These individuals want help without truly believing or trusting God. They want God to change them without correcting them. They do not want to leave the flesh. Even though their flesh is painful, they protect it with all of the inner defenses they have. When Jesus ministered healing and mercy, the crowds eagerly received. They pursued Him to receive more material blessings after He fed the five thousand. But when He said He was the bread of heaven and that to have life they would have to eat His flesh and drink His blood—to receive and believe Him and to live in a dependent relationship to Him—there was a separation.

> As a result of this many of His disciples withdrew, and were not walking with Him any more. Jesus said therefore to the twelve, "You do not want to go away also, do you?"
> Simon Peter answered Him, "Lord, to whom shall we go? You have words of eternal life. And we have believed and have come to know that You are the Holy One of God." (John 6:66-69)

Although many people eagerly received the teachings and counsel of Jesus, there came a time when His followers were given the choice to deny themselves, take up the cross, and follow Him. He recognized that not all people would receive His love and His Word.

> And He spoke many things to them in parables, saying, "Behold, the sower went out to sow; and as he sowed, some seeds fell beside the road, and the birds came and devoured them. And others fell upon the rocky places, where they did not have much soil; and immediately they sprang up, because they had no depth of soil. But when the sun had risen, they were scorched; and because they had no root, they withered away. And others fell among the thorns, and the thorns came up and choked them out. And others fell on the good soil, and yielded a crop, some a hundredfold, some sixty, and some thirty. (Matthew 13:3-8)

When Jesus explained the spiritual significance of the parable, He revealed that although the same seed is planted by the same sower in the same manner, the receptivity of the soil determined the amount of fruit-bearing. Likewise in counseling, one may sow the same seed (truth) in the same manner (mercy), but the response of the person will vary. Some ground is very hard, but the ministry of love may soften the soil. Others may quickly and eagerly try new ways of thinking and acting, discontinue counseling, and drift away from the church. Again, others may be entangled constantly in problems and barely grow into Christian maturity. Of course, those who are the most rewarding to the biblical counselor are those who receive the seed and bear much fruit.

Great patience is needed in counseling because people do not usually change overnight with a bit of advice and a prayer. In fact, a counselor may need to provide the environment of love while the person's soil is being broken up, or while the stones are being removed, or while the thorns and briars are being cut away. A spiritual counselor needs to be persistent in mercy, patience, and prayer.

Jesus told another parable about the sower and the seed:

> The kingdom of heaven may be compared to a man who sowed good seed in his field. But while men were sleeping, his enemy came and sowed tares also among the wheat, and went away. But when the wheat sprang up and bore grain, then the tares became evident also. And the slaves of the landowner came and said to him, "Sir, did you not sow good seed in your field? How then does it have tares?"
>
> And he said to them, "An enemy has done this!"

And the slaves said to him, "Do you want us, then, to go and gather them up?"

But he said, "No; lest while you are gathering up the tares, you may root up the wheat with them. Allow both to grow together until the harvest; and in the time of the harvest I will say to the reapers, 'First gather up the tares; and bind them in bundles to burn them up; but gather the wheat into my barn.' " (Matthew 13:24-30)

The church is to care for all who are within its walls. All are to be given the benefits of the same environment of mercy, kindness, forgiveness, and love. All are to be given the water of the Word and spiritual direction. The church should provide preaching, teaching, and counseling to each person who has chosen to be part of the visible church. We are not called to decide who is a tare and who is wheat, but rather to minister mercy and truth to all who align themselves with Christian fellowship.

Not all Christians seek biblical counseling. Because of the promises offered by psychological counseling, some Christians will choose the psychological way. But the church should offer biblical counseling to those in the body who are suffering from problems of living. If the church refers to psychologists persons who desire to mature spiritually through problems of living, it is not providing the means of healing, personal concern, and growth within the body. We tell people about the counseling ministry in our church, but they are free to choose biblical counseling within the body or psychological counseling within the community. If they choose the psychological way and ask the pastoral staff for names of professional counselors, the pastors say that since biblical counseling is provided by the church no referrals are made to psychological counselors.

Counseling is not always the answer for people experiencing emotional turmoil or problems. Not all people are responsive to counseling. Also, a number of studies indicate that people can improve without any kind of counseling. Nevertheless, most people have been conditioned to think that if someone is having problems or is experiencing any kind of emotional disturbance, that person needs counseling. In actuality, some may benefit more from the caring of a small group. Most will benefit from a kind, understanding friend who knows how to listen.

21. *Extent of ministry.* The pastor and church leaders need to determine what kinds of problems and the depth of severity of

problems that will be handled by the counseling staff. Although a church may decide to minister to the whole range of problems, including individuals taking antipsychotic medication under the care of a medical doctor, a church may only want to minister to those with problems of living that are not complicated by serious biological involvement.

It is helpful to establish guidelines for areas of specialities, such as financial counseling, marriage counseling, and premarital counseling. Certain counselors are effective with certain kinds of problems. Some counselors may prefer to counsel only in the area of family finance. Others may prefer to counsel couple-to-couple in marriage and/or premarital counseling. Some counselors may have a burden for one type of problem, such as homosexuality or living with an unsaved spouse. Also there may be some in the congregation who have seen the Lord minister in certain difficult circumstances in their own lives, such as the death of a child, who are willing to minister to others who are in the midst of similar situations.

The leadership also needs to decide the population to be served by the church counseling ministry. We have found that because counseling is a body ministry it is best to minister only to those within the local fellowship. These are our reasons:

a. Those who have a vital involvement in the local fellowship not only find help during counseling, but also grow spiritually through other areas of ministry.

b. Within the context of a local body an individual can avail himself of teaching in the Word, prayer, personal support, and a continuation of help through the various ministries within the church.

c. When an individual merely comes for counseling, he may not be receiving the support and ministry and encouragement he could from other ministries in the church.

d. When an individual is committed to a fellowship of believers and receiving counseling from within that loving and caring environment, he is more apt to take upon himself his share of the responsibility to change and grow.

e. Since the counseling is really part of the body life, one who comes in from the outside once a week misses out on receiving the ministry within that context.

f. Limiting the ministry to those who are or will become part of
    the fellowship will reduce confusion of doctrine. This reason is
    related to the thinking behind our decision to discourage
    counselees from seeking professional counseling. If a person is
    hearing one message at church and another one in counseling,
    he may be receiving more confusion than would be helpful in
    his present state of problems. We believe that counseling
    operates most effectively when it is part of the local church
    ministry.

22. *Inform church members about the counseling ministry.* Once the
counseling ministry is set up, the pastor may wish to describe the
ministry to the congregation. Or he may merely wish to refer those
who are in need of help to the counseling ministry. Other vehicles
for information would be the church bulletin and church newsletter.
Small-group leaders should be informed of the ministry as well.

YOUR CHURCH

The foregoing organizational suggestions are just that: suggestions. A counseling ministry must be designed by each individual
body in order to best serve that fellowship. The counseling ministry
is not to be an addition nailed onto the outside of the church. Nor is
your church to conform itself to another church's design for a
counseling ministry. Rather, such a ministry should be part of the
very fabric of the church. Though it is spiritual, it should be the
natural response of the body to the needs of its members. In fact, a
church need not even call this a counseling ministry with "counselors" and "counselees." A church could refer to the ministry with
whatever designation that would be the most appropriate for that
body. Some churches call it "shepherding," others "discipling." The
Lord will lead in this endeavor as the body prays and seeks His will
through His Word and His Holy Spirit.

Although human beings are complex, biblical counseling is not
as difficult as one might suppose. The basic elements are these: the
Lord Himself along with His Word and His love; the counselee who
desires change and will take responsibility in a dependent relationship with the Lord; a counselor who is well grounded in the Word,
who is walking consistently with the Lord, and who ministers the
Lord's love through a balance of mercy and truth.

When Jesus asked Peter, "Do you love Me?" He coupled his question with the command "Feed My sheep." He did not say, "Send My sheep over to another pasture." Jesus also said:

> I came that they might have life, and might have it abundantly. I am the good shepherd; the good shepherd lays down His life for the sheep. (John 10:10-11)

The life Jesus gives comes through His Word, His Holy Spirit, and His visible Body, the church. The church is called, anointed, and empowered to give His life and His love to all who come with needs. What the Lord has provided through His Word, His Holy Spirit, and His church is adequate for establishing and maintaining mental-emotional-behavioral health as well as spiritual health. Rather than running after the psychological way and amalgamating its divergent systems, the church needs to return to the biblical, spiritual way and to reestablish the cure-of-souls ministry. Jesus has given us the way to mental, emotional, and spiritual healing.

> Blessed is the man that walketh not
> in the counsel of the ungodly, nor
> standeth in the way of sinners, nor
> sitteth in the seat of the scornful.
>   But his delight is in the law of the
> Lord; and in his law doth he meditate
> day and night.
>   And he shall be like a tree planted by
> the rivers of water, that bringeth
> forth his fruit in his season; his leaf
> also shall not wither; and whatsoever
> he doeth shall prosper.
>   (Psalm 1:1-3, KJV)

Conclusion

In *The Psychological Way/The Spiritual Way* we defined psychological counseling as "a limited (one to one), timed (50 minutes), fixed (one day a week), paid ($25–$75 per hour), routine (one right after another) relationship [that] leaves little room for depth or creativity."[1] In each of these elements there is a dramatic difference between psychological counseling and biblical counseling.

Limited (one to one): Psychological counseling provides one therapist to see one person or a couple for purposes of help. Biblical counseling encourages the involvement of others in the congregation to provide continued friendship and also special help at times of need. There are times in biblical counseling when a counselee is surrounded by several individuals who pray for and encourage the person in need of help. In biblical counseling more than one person can be turned to if help is needed.

Timed (50 minutes): The professional practitioner must cram his appointments into an even flow of individuals for the sake of his own convenience and income. The length of time is for the benefit of the therapist and not the counselee. One individual said her therapist had a light bulb that flickered five minutes before the end of the 50-minute "hour." Is the psychological counselor likely to give a highly

1. Martin Bobgan and Deidre Bobgan, *The Psychological Way/The Spiritual Way* (Minneapolis: Bethany Fellowship, 1979), p. 159.

distraught counselee more than the 50 minutes alloted him on the counselor's crammed calendar? Or, conversely, is the psychological counselor likely to end a session after 15 minutes if he can extend the session and be paid for 50 minutes? The biblical counselor can meet as little as a few minutes or for as long as the circumstances require.

Fixed (one day a week): Psychological counselors rarely see counselees outside the office setting. In fact, certain psychological approaches discourage such meetings. Friendships between counselors and counselees are limited by the time period between on-the-hour to ten-minutes-to-the-hour. Any additional meetings add to the cost of the relationship and are usually an inconvenience to the counselor, who must disrupt his prescribed week or interrupt his weeknight or weekend time. The biblical counselor has a greater latitude of availability because there is no demand of thirty to fifty other individuals needing his attention. Counselees with extreme problems are encouraged to call at any time if the situation warrants it.

Paid ($25–$75 per hour): Many have come to the conclusion that a professional counselor is merely a paid friend. The cruelty of that description is overlooked as people smile at it. What kind of an individual must be paid to sustain friendship? In professional counseling, if the bill is not paid, the relationship is not continued. A paid relationship would be justified if psychotherapy were a science and if its trained practitioners did any better than untrained individuals. But psychotherapy is not a science, and it has not been proved that professionals do better than nonprofessionals. The motivation of money shall continue to sustain the practice of psychotherapy, but without justification. Biblical counseling is a ministry that cannot be purchased with money.

Routine (one right after another): The flow of patients in and out of a psychotherapist's office is the inevitable result of the therapist's need to produce a good income. Money requires patients, and more money requires more patients. The counselee can calculate the number of others who preceded him and the number that will follow based upon his own appointment time. The influx and efflux of clients and the numbers involved to sustain a profitable practice can only lead to mediocrity of results. There is no one-right-after-another parade in biblical counseling because it is a shared ministry within the Body of Christ.

In addition to the above shortcomings of psychological counseling and those mentioned in earlier chapters, there are numerous others. We mention only a few.

Sickness. Psychological counselors tend to think in terms of sickness. When they confront mental-emotional-behavioral problems they view them as diseases. The very term *mental illness* reveals this attitude. Although some therapists are no longer using this term there is still a strong tendency to think and treat people with problems as patients with pathologies. The biblical counselor does not view sin as sickness. Instead he sees problems of living as possibilities for spiritual growth and looks for remedies and resolutions in the spiritual realm.

Wisdom of men. Sigmund Freud, Alfred Adler, Carl Jung, B. F. Skinner, Carl Rogers, and numerous others have used their own wisdom to devise explanations for why people behave as they do and to give suggested solutions as to how people can change. Over 250 approaches and over 10,000 techniques in psychological counseling testify to the confusion in the field. With so many divergent remedies for the same problems one wonders why the psychological empire has not already collapsed from its own contradictions. The biblical counselor uses the Bible as his main reference point. If real, lasting, eternally worthy change is to occur it must be at the spiritual level. Tuning one's mind, will, emotions, and actions to the wisdom of men will lead to confidence in the flesh. But conforming one's mind, will, emotions, and actions to the wisdom of God will lead to a deeper relationship with the Creator and will bring one closer to being conformed to the image of Christ. Other books, including great literature, are not avoided. But when it comes to the knowledge of men and power for change, these writings must be subservient to God's Word.

One-up. Psychological counseling has often been referred to as a "one-up" relationship. It is obvious that the one up is the counselor. What is equally obvious, but not often stated, is that the counselee is in a one-down position. This one-up, one-down relationship is characteristic of psychological counseling. On the other hand, biblical counseling is a relationship of equality. Both the counselor and counselee are equal before the cross of Christ. This equality provides a fertile ground for the relationship and for possible growth. The counselee needs to know that there is only One who can be in the one-up position, and He is the One who both created mankind and then humbled Himself to a most horrible one-down position in order to give people an opportunity to stand with the One who truly is in the one-up position.

Science. The false facade of science behind which psychotherapy has hidden for many years has now been exposed by many writers. Directly or indirectly, overtly or covertly, psychotherapy involves values and morals and therefore is a religious activity. Some psychotherapists are brave enough to admit that, but others prefer to disguise it. The biblical counselor knows that counseling is a religious activity. Therefore he finds his model and methodology of change in Scripture. The ingredients of faith, hope, and love are both admitted and encouraged in biblical counseling.

Self-love. Psychotherapy fosters self-love in a great variety of ways. Most psychological theories are humanistic in their solutions to life's problems. In one way or another, almost all psychotherapy lifts up man, rather than God, as the great I Am. We have emphasized that Satan's temptation and man's Fall reveal a vulnerability of man to self-exaltation. The flesh consistently cries out for godhood. The biblical counselor recognizes this downward pull of the flesh and counters it with the upward lift of the Spirit and the Word.

THE PSYCHOLOGICAL WAY OR THE SPIRITUAL WAY

When there is a breakdown in relationships, when there are family problems, when there is a problem with anger, fear, or any other disabling human emotion, the answer is found in God's love, not in man's wisdom. Biblical, not psychological, principles speak to man's true condition and to man's true needs for transformation. Whereas worldly wisdom prevails in the professional counseling realm, God's point of view prevails in a biblical approach to humanity.

Although it may be difficult to believe in the spiritual way to mental-emotional healing during this current age of psychological preoccupation, the cure-of-souls ministry is a crucial need today. Believers have at their disposal the most powerful weapons and tools for change that have ever been known by man, but the church has overlooked them. Simply leading an individual into a closer relationship with God and a deeper spiritual experience will have more transforming power than any psychotherapy. No knowledge of psychotherapy is necessary to transform human lives, only a knowledge of the Word, experience in walking in the Spirit, and a gift to minister this Word and this life to another person.

Biblical counseling within a fellowship of believers ministers to the whole person not only through conversation, but through action. Through the resources of the church members, a counseling ministry can provide practical things such as family budget counseling, help with household moving, groceries for those in need, help in seeking a job, referral to local colleges or schools, rides when needed, suggestions for baby-sitting, referral to good child-care centers, arrangements for help with homework for children, and much more, depending upon the need.

Psychotherapists do not have the time necessary to provide for such needs, nor are they equipped to help individuals in these ways in most cases. Psychotherapy cannot minister to the whole person. In addition to the limitations mentioned earlier, it is limited by conversation. The only help given is through talking and listening. In other words, the therapist cannot be a real friend to the counselee and cannot meet his broader needs.

In chapter 2 we mentioned the research of Leonard Syme, Professor of Epidemiology at the University of California at Berkeley. His research related social ties with disease and death rates. Social ties are important and apparently lead to better health and longevity. Spiritual ties are even more important because they are at the deepest and most significant level of man. Those individuals who have the benefit of a spiritual support system are best able to endure the heartaches and headaches of life and to properly enjoy the good times. A spiritual support group, which might include a spouse (if one is married), a family, a church, or a small Christian fellowship, and friends can provide an environment of love so necessary for withstanding problems.

In chapter 5 we presented research showing that addictive behaviors such as smoking, overeating, and alcohol and drug abuse are best overcome by the individual himself, and that the least effective way of dealing with these problems is individual professional therapy. Help can best occur by the use of informal biblical support, the sanctuary worship service, and person-to-person relationships. The church carries the responsibility to provide opportunities for such guidance and support. The entire body is to be working together in such a manner that believers are drawn closer to God and into maturity in Christ. Because growth is to occur within the Body of Christ, and since growth comes from one's personal relationship with God, biblical counselors will encourage participation in groups and friendship in the church and will also encourage personal responsibility in relationship to God.

Even if a church does not have nor does not care to begin a counseling ministry, the least that church can do is to provide an environment where Christians are encouraged to form spiritual ties with one another. The least a pastor can do is to establish small groups within the church that are centered on Bible study, prayer, and living the Christian life. Quite often the cure of souls is a natural outgrowth of small-group ministry within the church fellowship.

Without even instituting a counseling ministry a pastor can refocus the attention from liturgy to love. Love has sustaining and transforming power, and churches need to provide an environment in which the person-to-person spiritual relationship can be maximized. All of the fellowship and all of the relationship is for the individual to know the love of God, to be transformed by it daily, and to be expressing that love to God and others. A spiritual fellowship that follows the Great Commandment will be the best antidote for the problems of life.

We encourage those who have a mental-emotional-behavioral need to seek help in their church; we urge those who have a call on their heart and a gift to do it to encourage their minister to develop a counseling ministry; and we appeal to ministers to begin such a ministry in their churches. The cure-of-souls ministry has existed in the church from its inception and has helped put people at peace with themselves, with their family and neighbor, and with God. The ministry of biblical counseling needs to be restored immediately so that the law of God (love) might be fulfilled.

Counseling as it is presently known and practiced must come to an end so that there might be a beginning of real help. The help, however, must be biblical—one that rests upon the Word of God and the work of the Holy Spirit. We need the kind of help that existed in the early church, in which believers truly bore one another's burdens and so fulfilled the law of Christ. We need to stop emulating professional counseling with its limited, timed, fixed, paid, routine, one-up, one-down system of cash flow from person to therapist, and to restore once more the caring community that should be a part of every church that names the name of Jesus.

We continue to have the hope with which we concluded *The Psychological Way/The Spiritual Way:*

> We believe that the Lord fully intends to restore the ministry of the cure of souls to the church. He will use both ministers and lay believers who will stand on the completeness of the Word of God. They will minister under the anointing of God's Holy Spirit and rely on God's principles outlined in His Word. They will operate as a priesthood of all believers and minister God's love, God's grace, God's mercy, God's faithfulness, and God's wisdom to those who are suffering from mental-emotional hurts and problems. They will voluntarily give of their time, their love, and their prayers to lift the heavy burdens. They will fulfill Paul's admonition: "Brethren, if a man be overtaken in a fault, ye which are spiritual, restore such an one in the spirit of meekness; considering thyself, lest thou also be tempted. Bear one another's burdens, and so fulfill the law of Christ. (Galatians 6:1-2, KJV)[2]

The source for counseling is the Lord Himself.

> If any man is thirsty, let him come to Me and drink. He who believes in Me, as the Scripture said, "From his innermost being shall flow rivers of living water." (John 7:37-38)

God has supplied the church with living water to meet the needs of every believer as he endures the trials of life. He urges His people to seek Him, not the wisdom of men:

> "Ho! Every one who thirsts, come to the waters;
> And you who have no money come, buy and eat.
> Come, buy wine and milk
> Without money and without cost.
> Why do you spend money for what is not bread,
> And your wages for what does not satisfy?
> Listen carefully to Me, and eat what is good,
> And delight yourself in abundance.
> Incline your ear and come to Me.
> Listen, that you may live. . . .
> For My thoughts are not your thoughts,
> Neither are your ways My ways," declares the Lord.
> "For as the heavens are higher than the earth,

---

2. Ibid., p. 203.

So are My ways higher than your ways,
And My thoughts than your thoughts."
(Isaiah 55:1-3, 8-9)

Jesus Christ is the answer to life's problems!

Selected Bibliography

Adams, Jay E. *A Christian Counselor's Manual.* Nutley, N.J.: Presb. & Ref., 1973; Grand Rapids: Baker, 1974.

———. *The Language of Counseling.* Phillipsburg, N.J.: Presb. & Ref., 1981; Grand Rapids: Baker, 1981.

———. *More Than Redemption.* Grand Rapids: Baker, 1979; Phillipsburg, N.J.: Presb. & Ref., 1979.

———. *Ready to Restore: A Layman's Guide to Christian Counseling.* Grand Rapids: Baker, 1981; Phillipsburg, N.J.: Presb. & Ref., 1981.

———. *The Use of Scriptures in Counseling.* Nutley, N.J.: Presb. & Ref., 1975; Grand Rapids: Baker, 1976.

Bobgan, Martin, and Deidre Bobgan. *The Psychological Way/The Spiritual Way.* Minneapolis: Bethany House, 1979.

Brownback, Paul. *The Danger of Self Love.* Chicago: Moody, 1982.

Christenson, Larry. *The Christian Family.* Minneapolis: Bethany House, 1970.

———. *The Renewed Mind.* Minneapolis: Bethany House, 1974.

Gross, Martin L. *The Psychological Society.* New York: Random, 1978.

Hinman, Nelson E. *An Answer to Humanistic Psychology.* Eugene, Oreg.: Harvest, 1980.

Hunt, Dave, and Tom McMahon. *The Seduction of Christianity.* Eugene, Oreg.: Harvest, 1984.

Keller, Phillip. *Taming Tension.* New York: Vantage, 1978.

Kilpatrick, William. *Psychological Seduction.* Nashville: Thomas Nelson, 1983.

Mack, Wayne. *A Homework Manual for Biblical Counseling.* Vols. 1 and 2. Phillipsburg, N.J.: Presb. & Ref., 1979 and 1980.

———. *How to Develop Deep Unity in the Marriage Relationship.* Phillipsburg, N.J.: Presb. & Ref., 1977.

Myers, David. *The Inflated Self: Human Illusions and the Biblical Call to Hope.* New York: Seabury, 1980.

Szasz, Thomas. *The Myth of Psychotherapy: Mental Healing as Religion, Rhetoric, and Repression.* Garden City, N.Y.: Doubleday, Anchor, 1978.

Tavris, Carol. *Anger: The Misunderstood Emotion.* New York: Simon & Schuster, 1983.

Torrey, E. Fuller. *The Death of Psychiatry.* Radnor, Pa.: Chilton, 1974.

Vitz, Paul. *Psychology as Religion: The Cult of Self-Worship.* Grand Rapids: Eerdmans, 1977.

Zilbergeld, Bernie. *The Shrinking of America: Myths of Psychological Change.* Boston: Little, Brown, 1983.

Index of Subjects

Index of Persons

Index of Scriptures

Moody Press, a ministry of the Moody Bible Institute, is designed for education, evangelization, and edification. If we may assist you in knowing more about Christ and the Christian life, please write us without obligation: Moody Press, c/o MLM, Chicago, IL 60610.